A man who is good enough to shed his blood for his country is good enough to be given a square deal afterwards.

—Theodore Roosevelt

Front cover: Horst Przybilski and Ike Refice
exchange greetings and memories.

Back Cover:

Herman Herrera and family

John D. Dingell   Eddie Taylor   Kathy Jo Benabides

PORTRAITS OF SERVICE

Looking into the Faces of Veterans

Robert H. Miller and Andrew Wakeford

PORTRAITS OF SERVICE™

Looking into the Faces of Veterans

For more information please contact the authors:
Robert H. Miller
rmiller@portraitsofus.org
Andrew Wakeford
awakeford@portraitsofus.org

Book Design: Nancy Rabitoy, Robert H. Miller, and Andrew Wakeford
Editor: Penny Schreiber

 Visit our book website: www.portraitsofservice.com

PATTON
★★★★
PUBLISHING
Post Office Box 482
New Hope, PA 18938
Phone: (215) 297-5747
PattonPublishing.com

ver.1700007202012rhm10k
Printed in China

President Barack Obama with veterans at the sixty-fifth anniversary commemoration of D-Day, at Omaha Beach, June 6, 2009.

Dedicated to those who fell

Photo Robert H. Miller

Table of Contents

A MESSAGE FROM HELEN PATTON,

granddaughter of General George S. Patton Jr.

The first-hand accounts revealed within these pages offer a rare glimpse into both the nobility and the horror of war. The faces of these men and women, who were given to service in the name of freedom, bear permanent witness to their humanity and to their pain. Photographers Robert H. Miller and Andrew Wakeford have captured their images with stunning delicacy. The expression on the face of each veteran contains a lifetime.

Yet for each individual profiled here, thousands more are no longer with us. They are not here to tell us their stories, and we can only dare to imagine their experiences.

As a representative of a family that's blessed with a military heritage spanning three hundred years on both sides, I have gazed into the faces of thousands of veterans. I have done my best to acknowledge their experiences and to assure them that they will most certainly be remembered.

I am founder of the Patton Foundation in America and the Patton Sustainable Trust in Europe and also head of Patton Publishing. Through these roles, I have dedicated myself to making sure our brave and committed veterans continue to be "seen." I am committing a portion of the proceeds from this book to benefit those who have more than earned the right to enjoy their share of the peace they secured for all of us.

Whether you have selected *Portraits of Service* to enhance your own library or that of a friend, you will be widening an important circle of awareness and compassion with your purchase of this tribute to the veterans of the world.

Many thanks,

Helen Patton
Chairman
The Patton Foundation

O woe is me. To have seen what I have seen; see what I see.

—Hamlet

Helen Patton, on Utah Beach, in Normandy, France.

Introducing . . .

Robert H. Miller

Mine has been a truly remarkable journey, beginning with the introduction of my first book, *Finding My Father's War*, in October 2009 (republished as *Hidden Hell* by Patton Publishing in June, 2011). Since then, I have spent much time in Europe promoting my book and meeting new people from all walks of life. Many are veterans with harrowing stories of survival from the wars in which they served. I have been fortunate to meet veterans from many wars, heads of state from four countries, and mayors and dignitaries from sleepy little towns in France, England, and Germany. Every World War II story I have heard has left an indelible impression on me. I will remember all of them forever.

On June 5, 2009, I had the great good luck of meeting Helen Patton on Utah Beach in Normandy, France, during the sixty-fifth anniversary commemoration of D-Day. Helen is the granddaughter of the iconic World War II general George S. Patton, and she has spent most of her adult life carrying forward the concerns for soldiers and veterans that her father, George S. Patton IV (also an army general), and grandfather shared. I humbly shook her hand on that day and instantly knew she was someone very special. Helen's caring, confidence, and passion clearly radiate from her heart. Her deep concern for and commitment to veterans of all wars is unwavering—part of her core DNA. I believe to this day that our meeting was not a chance encounter, but destiny.

Because of Helen's efforts the name "Patton" still rings strong throughout Europe. After visiting her Stiftung Foundation in Germany on numerous occasions, attending several veterans' memorial celebrations in France, and making one special trip to visit with the entire Patton family at their Green Meadows Farm north of Boston, I now find myself immersed in and committed to the newly formed Patton Foundation here in America.

I have been named its first executive director, and I am deeply honored and grateful to have been asked by Helen Patton to represent and lead her foundation. I know the task ahead of me is a daunting one, but I look forward to putting into practice General George S. Patton's concern for the welfare of American soldiers and their families. I also anticipate with excitement meeting many more veterans.

My association with Helen Patton has also resulted in my meeting Andrew Wakeford, who serves as the project manager at Patton Stiftung. Andrew and I are both seasoned professional photographers, and it did not take long for us to establish a strong friendship. Within months, driven by a shared passion and a burning desire to make a difference, we came up with the idea of photographing veterans from all recent wars. Combining our shared interests in photography and writing, we set as our goal the creation of a book centering on veterans. *Portraits of Service: Looking into the Faces of Veterans* will be the result of our combined efforts, and I am very proud to have embarked on this project with Andrew.

In conclusion, I am honored to walk in the shadows of all the veterans in the world. War is an unfortunate by-product of human disagreement. It is fortunate, though, that at times of war men and women have responded and been willing to make the personal sacrifices necessary for all of us to live in freedom. Our book takes a cross section of veterans from many countries and gives them the opportunity to express themselves as they wish. Although it is not possible to photograph every veteran, it is our hope to capture the thoughts and feelings of those we do photograph and convey the importance of what they have done on behalf of humanity. It is a pleasure for me to be a part of this book.

Photo Andrew Wakeford

Andrew Wakeford

As a resident of Germany for over thirty years, having moved to Saarbrücken from my home in Britain, it was interesting for me to recently discover that Helen Patton, granddaughter of the famous general, also lived in the same area of Saarland, one of the smallest of all German "Länder." It is historically appropriate for her to live in the place where her grandfather, General George S. Patton Jr., had predicted that the outcome of World War II would be decided. We met and soon became friends. Since then I have been privileged to meet all sorts of people who I would otherwise probably never have met: actors, musicians, World War II death-march survivors, film directors, film producers, authors, ambassadors, ministers, psychiatrists, psychologists, nuns, monks, abbesses, active soldiers, theater producers, rabbis, war veterans, and the writer and photographer Robert Miller, who had met Helen during the 2009 D-Day commemorations. Miller has written a moving book about his father's experience as a POW in Germany.

When Robert approached me with the idea of the two of us taking photographs of veterans for book publication, I was all for it. I've always found my experiences with veterans fascinating, and I thought it would be a tremendous photographic challenge. Each and every war veteran has stories to tell of human bravery and kindness, weakness and strength, despair and hope, sadness and joy. Probably they are much like any life story we may be privileged to hear, but veterans' stories share a unique intensity. Many have lived their full adult lives before deciding to open up and talk about what happened to them during their wars. The zeitgeist of these past times often seemed to take on a palpable energy in our conversations and became a lesson in observation for both my ears and my eyes.

Meeting and photographing veterans has been an incredibly rewarding experience, and I would in some ways describe it as the most unusual assignment I have ever taken on. While friendship between soldiers of the same company may be considered a given, it also can extend outward to those from other countries, some of whom were in fact former enemies. It is a strange fact that has revealed itself to me that no matter how deep the enmity between them may have been, it can in time become an irrelevance, or just an interesting aspect of life which later turns itself inside out through our common humanity. The bottom line seems to be that we can love and respect our supposed enemies if we can only get to know one another. A conflict can only take place when we are not sufficiently informed about each other, and it escalates on the dubious basis of what we have been told. Then war is employed as a weapon of last resort, used either to fight against someone's freedom or to defend our own.

The men and women in this book understand that they were but cogs in a machine when a challenge presented itself, the challenge perhaps of a seemingly unstoppable force. The random group we are showing here represents millions who have fought and countless others who have lost their lives. Some in this group are famous, some are anonymous, and many are in-between, but they all share the experience of service to their country in the cause of war. There is no agenda for these images and they are not anti-war or pro-war; war is a human experience that sometimes takes place when we have lost or given up on other methods of negotiating. But these images suggest to us that we must look at and think about what soldiers do in our name. We must remember that they have represented us and risked their lives for us and not ignore the unpleasant facts of history as we go about our daily routines. If we spend a few moments looking at a picture of a veteran contemplating his active service, we will have offered him the understanding and respect that we all owe to one another.

Photo Christa Wakeford

It's like I was walking, walking through a dream
Where nothing ever happened to me
But brother I got scars, I got scars no man can see

—"Scars," lyrics by Darden Smith and Jordan Dailey

With lyrics straight from the heart of those who have been to war, Faces of Freedom seeks to build awareness and support for wounded warrior empowerment programs.

http://itunes.apple.com/us/album/faces-of-freedom-ep/id460671403

Photographs of Veterans

JESSICA GOODELL

She helped to retrieve, identify, and process fallen marines

Deployment: Iraq
Served: U.S. Marines, Mortuary Affairs Unit
Nationality: American
Residence: Buffalo, New York
Occupation: Author, graduate student

"Sometimes we had to scoop up the remains with our hands or retrieve limbs and place it all into a body bag."

Jessica Goodell, twenty-eight, is soft spoken and eloquent. Her Iraq War experience is almost impossible for anyone to fully comprehend. Her beautiful eyes become dull and lifeless the moment she begins to tell her story of serving in the Mortuary Affairs Unit of the United States Marines.

"It was our job to do the work of retrieving the remains of fallen Marines. We were also responsible for identifying the bodies and preparing them to be sent home to their families," she explains. "I was involved with this work for nine months, from February to November 2004."

Goodell wore a hazmat suit when she was called to a scene where Marines were reported down. Her job was typically unpredictable, dangerous, and horrific. "We were prepared for almost anything," she recalls. In Iraq soldiers often died as the result of an explosion, and in most cases, says Goodell, they would not find a clean body on the ground.

"Sometimes it is a little more messy," she says. The hazmat suit protected her from the effects of exploded bodies that were no longer intact. "Sometimes we had to scoop up the remains with our hands or retrieve limbs and place it all into a body bag," she recalls. "It is so important to collect everything, as much as possible, so that the family can know that they have all of their loved one's remains."

Goodell explains that there is a distinct difference between the feel of body bags containing intact bodies and the ones that contain shattered remains: "The shattered remains just slide together in the center of the bag when it is lifted." She also remembers the stench of death: "For nine months it was on everything we owned. It permeated our skin and became the permanent smell inside our noses. It also caused us to not want to eat. We all struggled with eating. It was incredibly hard."

Goodell recalls this sad experience from the early days of her deployment with Mortuary Affairs:

We had a call that a marine was down and some of the soldiers would be bringing him to us for processing. When the body arrived it was whole and pretty much intact. My aide was busy getting the hands on the top of the body in preparation for fingerprinting. Suddenly, he said, 'Goodell, you might want to look at this.' When I looked, the arms were moving very fluidly and easily. Normally this is not the case. I looked at the marine's chest, and I watched it slowly rise and fall. Alarmed, we immediately notified our Sir [officer]. He came over and saw what we were experiencing and quickly summoned the doctor on duty. He came over to our station and examined the body. After a long, uneasy pause, he said, 'there is nothing we can do right now for this marine. We just have to wait.' I imagine now that it must have been a situation where nothing could have been done. But at the time, I just couldn't imagine waiting. I said quietly to myself over and over again: 'Wait for what? *Wait for what?*'

The marine slowly died, and they proceeded with processing his remains.

Today Goodell is a graduate student studying to become a clinical psychotherapist specializing in trauma, with a focus on veterans. Her book *Shade It Black: Death and After in Iraq* is about her nine months with the Mortuary Affairs Unit.

ALEXANDER JEFFERSON

Supporting the honor of the Tuskegee Airmen

Deployment: World War II, Europe
Served: U.S. Army Air Corps (Tuskegee Airmen)
Nationality: American
Residence: Southfield, Michigan
Occupation: Retired elementary school teacher

"Back in the 1940s I knew I was being discriminated against, but I would not let that hold me back from achieving my goals in life."

Alexander Jefferson is so articulate and polished he could be mistaken for a professional speaker and presenter. Warm and friendly, the ninety-one-year-old is clearly a man who would never let anything get in the way of his dreams. He is a living legacy of his determination to succeed at all costs.

Born in 1921 in Detroit, Michigan, Jefferson grew up in the heart of the city. After high school, he attended Clark College in Atlanta, Georgia, where he majored in chemistry and biology. After graduation he joined the U.S. Army Reserve and enrolled in graduate school at Howard University in Washington, DC. It was not long before he was called to active duty to serve in World War II. "That's when it all changed for me," says Jefferson. He enrolled in advanced flight training at the Tuskegee Army Airfield. "There were nine hundred men just like me—all of us were part of the black air force," he says.

After extensive training, Jefferson was sent to Italy. He flew missions to Germany and France, escorting B-17 and B-24 bombers. "On my nineteenth mission near the coast of France my job was to knock out the German radar stations just prior to the D-Day invasion," recalls Jefferson. "I remember it clearly—the shell came up through the floor into the cockpit just missing me. I ejected and landed in the trees far below. As I parachuted down, the Germans were watching me all the way."

Jefferson was captured and became a POW. He was stunned to discover that the Germans seemed to know everything about him. "What amazed me—they knew about my college experience and some of my personal life," he says. "I have no idea to this day where they got that information." Jefferson was eventually transferred to Stalag Luft III, near the Polish border. "I was

there for about five months until we were hastily moved out," Jefferson recalls. "The Russians were approaching." Under heavy guard they walked eighty kilometers, eventually ending up in the horrific Stalag VIIA in the small town of Moosberg, Germany.

Jefferson had privileges as a pilot and an officer and was housed in a remote part of the camp. "My treatment was far different from most of the inhabitants in there. If you were in the infantry and ended up at Stalag VIIA, you were treated lower than scum," says Jefferson. "Because I was an officer—even a black officer—my treatment was superior, and I basically sat on my butt waiting for the war to end." Jefferson remembers General George S. Patton liberating the camp in April 1945.

Today the retired school teacher reflects on his long life:

I am so proud to have served for this great nation. Discrimination was a real problem during my younger days. But my parents taught me important lessons: to set goals and reach for your dreams, because nobody is going to get your dreams for you. That's exactly what I did. I would figure out different ways to get around the problems of life. I would never resort to feeling sorry for myself or making excuses because of my race. I live now fat, dumb, and happily retired and do whatever I can to support the honor of the Tuskegee Airmen.

Alexander Jefferson remains passionate and energetic and enjoys traveling the country as an honored member of the elite Tuskegee Airmen of World War II.

Photo Robert H. Miller

STEVEN KRAFT

Still struggling twenty years after Operation Desert Storm

Deployment: Kuwait, Saudi Arabia, Iraq
Served: U.S. Army
Nationality: American
Residence: Colorado Springs, Colorado
Occupation: Unemployed construction worker

One night after falling asleep Kraft dreamt that balloon people armed with AK-47s were shooting at him. He began to shoot back, and pretty soon everything turned real, with blood and guts everywhere.

Steven Kraft, forty-six, lives in the Crawford House shelter for the homeless in Colorado Springs, Colorado. He served in the U.S. Army during Operation Desert Storm, and he believes that Americans should have known more about the Arabic culture before going in. U.S. forces were trying to change a culture that had evolved over thousands of years, he says. It is his belief that the Americans weren't welcome over there to begin with, and the people of Kuwait changed back to their familiar ways, he says, after being liberated.

Kraft has no good memories of that time. A medic was kidnapped and later found beheaded. That was the moment when Kraft, then a young man of twenty-one, changed his outlook on everything. Steve and the medic had become friends during their training, and he had known the man's wife and newborn daughter.

The preparations for going to war were thorough, recalls Kraft, but much seemed woefully lacking when it came time to engage in real warfare on the battlefield. He remembers the first time he shot someone: it was an Iraqi he shot in the chest three times in the midst of a battle. On advancing forward afterward, he could see nothing was left of the man. Kraft's eyes reflect profound sadness as he explains his PTSD—the constant nightmares and the fearsome signs of alcohol abuse. For quite a long time alcohol was the only way he knew of covering up the experience of war. When Kraft returned home, he listened in shock as his grandmother said she didn't recognize him. Eventually his marriage of seventeen years ended, and his life fell apart in every other way.

Kraft says he has no regrets about joining the military, and even wishes he had remained in the army longer. But the war did him in. He worked in concrete construction afterward for twenty years, but sclerosis in his lower back, PTSD, arthritis, and intermittent problems with alcohol caused him to give up.

One night after falling asleep Kraft dreamt that balloon people armed with AK-47s were shooting at him. He began to shoot back, and pretty soon everything turned real, with blood and guts everywhere. He woke up in a cold sweat, and when he finally fell asleep again, the dream kicked off right where it had stopped, just like a movie. His sleep is frequently interrupted by violent nightmares and bad dreams, but often he forgets what they have been about, and he's just left with the feelings. He says he has fantastic support from Miss Vicky, the manager of Crawford House, who takes such great care of the veterans.

When interviewed for this profile, Steve Kraft had gone 222 days without alcohol and was still counting each day a special achievement.

Photo Andrew Wakeford

HERMAN HERRERA

The hazards of PTSD combined with too much medication and alcohol nearly led to disaster

Deployment: Iraq

Served: U.S. Army

Nationality: American

Residence: Visalia, Colorado

Occupation: Adventure coordinator, LifeQuest Transitions

"My Humvee was hit during my third deployment in Iraq. I guess that's what tipped me over the edge."

"My Humvee was hit during my third deployment in Iraq. I guess that's what tipped me over the edge."

Herman Herrera, thirty-two, and a father of two, begins to talk about the time he went over that edge. In February 2008, on a cold and rainy winter day in Baghdad, the Humvee he was riding in was hit by a heat-sensitive bomb. The reality of these bombs had been with Herrera since 2003, when they were still fairly primitive. But over time they became more sophisticated and deadly, he explains, and during his second deployment in Iraq, in 2006 and 2007, the bombs were a daily factor in his life. The attack on that fateful day in February 2008 finally took him beyond the breaking point.

Miraculously no one was hurt in the attack, although the back of the Humvee had been blown off. The crew was checked, deemed fit for duty, and sent back in. But for staff sergeant Herrera, that attack signaled for him how weary he was of living with frequent explosions, the shock of sudden overwhelming noise, and the terror of anticipating injury or death for himself or his comrades. This was enough for Herrera to go over the edge.

Several months later, in June, Herrera's unit was called up to aid in the push into Sadr City. They spent eighteen hours straight in combat every day for two weeks, enduring heavy machine-gun and small-arms fire, before being relieved. The temperature was about one hundred degrees outside, and much hotter inside the unit's Bradley tank. Herrera was horrified by the stress and torment he and his crew suffered as a result of those suffocating hours spent under random fire.

When Herrera returned to the U.S. early in 2009, his wife noticed that his mental health had deteriorated drastically. He was filled with raw anger, and she urged him to seek professional help. His wife made it clear to him that their marriage was on the line, and Herrera sought the help of a therapist. By September 2009 he was taking twelve drugs daily for PTSD, sleep problems, headaches, high blood pressure, anger issues, and bad dreams. His problems qualified him for thirty days of leave.

When he arrived home, his wife advised him to stop taking the dangerous cocktail of medicines. Feeling angry and confused, Herrera wondered why after telling him to get treatment she was now complaining about it. But he decided to take her advice and, without consulting his doctors, he went off his meds cold turkey. He immediately turned to alcohol and began to drink heavily. One night, after his wife and son had gone to bed, Herrera drank until he blacked out; he woke up in his garage. He heard himself say that he was going to go upstairs to kill his wife. "I didn't know how to cope with that," he says. The next day he told his wife what had happened and she became frightened, telling him to go to the hospital.

Herrera ignored her suggestion, and that night he drank alcohol, took sleeping pills, and left suicide notes around. He wrote to his wife that he was sorry and that she deserved better. She later found him alive and stayed with him to keep him from falling asleep.

The next day he agreed to be hospitalized and was admitted to a PTSD clinic away from the pressures of his family life. He eventually left the army and today works out regularly and is employed as an adventure counselor at LifeQuest Transitions, a nonprofit organization that serves wounded veterans. He believes his worst battles are behind him. Although Herrera still suffers from occasional nightmares, he lives an otherwise normal life.

Photo Andrew Wakeford

JOHN D. DINGELL

U.S. congressman

Deployment: World War II, Europe
Served: U.S. Army
Nationality: American
Residence: Dearborn, Michigan
Occupation: United States representative, Michigan's 15th Congressional District

"It was important to me that I receive the same treatment and bear the same burdens as the other men serving."

The words of John Dingell:

In 1944, I entered service in the Army because I wanted to serve my country and was eager to be a part of the war effort. At the time, my father, John D. Dingell Sr., served Michigan's Sixteenth District in the U.S. House of Representatives. Because it was important to me that I receive the same treatment and bear the same burdens as the other men serving, I always made a point to not mention my father's career during my time in the Army. I successfully kept it unknown except for one special instance. It was in April 1945, when Franklin Delano Roosevelt died.

FDR had led our nation for more than twelve years. The country was feeling alarmed with a real sense of uncertainty about how to continue as a nation without him during the latter days of World War II. After having looked to FDR for strong leadership for so long and entrusting our country to him to lead us, it was a scary time.

When he died, the vice president, Harry S. Truman, took command of the Armed Forces and began to lead the nation. Around that time, the men in my unit came to me as I was reading my mail. I looked up, and what seemed like the whole platoon was at the foot of my bunk. They said, 'Dingell, your dad's in Congress. Please tell us, who is this new man Truman and what sort of man is he?' I was surprised that they found out about my dad but told them I'd write to him and ask him. I did just that, and soon after I received a response. I read that letter aloud to the men serving with me and gave them my father's answer. He wrote that Truman was a great man, he would lead this nation ably, and we could depend on him.

My dad was right on. Harry Truman went on to become not just a great president and amazing visionary but a worthy successor to the mantle of leadership FDR had left him. Harry was a man who made tough decisions, not because they were easy but because they were right. From the White House to the front lines, World War II brought out the best in this nation and its people. I am extremely proud of the small role I played in that effort, and I am grateful and humbled for having been part of such a critical chapter in America's history.

Photo Robert H. Miller

Richard Brookins

A surprise call from Luxembourg thirty-three years later

Deployment: World War II, Europe
Served: U.S. Army
Nationality: American
Residence: Rochester, New York
Occupation: Communications engineer (retired)

"I had almost forgotten about this episode in my life. But to the people of Wiltz, in Luxembourg, the memories were still fresh."

In the fall of 1944, before the Battle of the Bulge began in earnest, American troops managed to enter Germany, which infuriated Hitler. As a result, the obscure and little-known Huertgen Forest became the scene of terrible casualties and fighting involving the Army's 28th Division. After two weeks of solid fighting and six-thousand casualties, the Division's Signal Corps was sent to regroup and rest at headquarters in the small town of Wiltz, in nearby Luxembourg. Richard Brookins, who today is ninety, was then the communications officer for the 28th.

The 28th arrived in Wiltz just before Thanksgiving. Brookins, the man responsible for offering the soldiers films on off days, got out his projector to show *Going My Way* as part of the Thanksgiving celebration. Harry Stutz, a buddy from the same unit, suggested to Brookins that the people of Wiltz might also like to celebrate. He had learned that an important annual event for the town, St. Nicholas Day, was coming soon, on December 5.

"We've been told not to fraternize," Brookins explained to his friend. But Stutz replied that the people of Luxembourg hated the Germans even more than the Americans did, and that they had been forced to join the German Wehrmacht. Those who'd resisted had been rounded up and shot. The German occupation of Luxembourg was now four years old, and there were children who had never experienced St. Nicholas Day, which had been celebrated in the region for hundreds of years.

Stutz managed to persuade Division commander General Cota that a party for the townspeople of Wiltz would not only raise their spirits but also be good for the morale of the troops who had suffered such devastating losses at Huertgen. Stutz visited the local priest to gain his enthusiastic support and went back to Brookins to persuade him to pose as St Nicholas, the star of the day.

On the day itself they found a bishop's robe for Brookins to wear, and it included a bishop's miter. The miter was a tight fit and gave him a mighty headache. But the children and townspeople hadn't experienced anything like this celebration for years. Here, in the middle of a war, was an American St. Nick in a jeep throwing candy and chocolate at the children and passing out doughnuts and presents. St. Nicholas Day in Wiltz was a huge success—it was filmed for a newsreel and covered by the Army publication *Stars and Stripes*.

Over thirty years later, in 1977, Richard Brookins received a surprise phone call from Wiltz, Luxembourg, inviting their first American St. Nick to return. Starting in 1945 the town had always given St. Nick a distinctive American flair and the townspeople had set up an organization to maintain the tradition and bring back the original.

Wiltz welcomed Richard Brookins back year after year until 2009, when he traveled to Luxembourg for the last time at age eighty-seven. Today Brookins remains proud that he was responsible for giving this town back the hope that had gone missing during the war.

This story was taken from The American St. Nick, *by Peter Lion, which is available from Patton Publishing.*

Photo Fred George

CHARLES

An inability to justify the horrors of war

Deployment: Peacekeeping in Somalia
Served: Army intelligence
Nationality: Undisclosed
Residence: Europe
Occupation: Undisclosed

*"I knew there were plenty of child soldiers in Africa, but I would never have thought
I would be confronted with them in this way."*

Charles is in his early forties and recovering from PTSD. He has managed to bring some stability to his life by moving away from a large city and finding solace in nature. In the 1990s his job in Somalia was to protect the transport of aid supplies for the civilian population in specific areas of conflict and famine. This was soon after the Black Hawk episode, and nerves were frayed as peacekeepers had their work cut out for them in trying to keep the peace. According to Charles:

> One clan was keen on stopping the transport of nutrition, tents, blankets, and medicine and redistributing the goods themselves. Of course they were the good guys for a while, as their own clan was sure of getting sufficient supplies. But anything that was left over they decided to sell, and with the money they earned, particularly for medicine, they bought weapons and ammunition.

Charles was working in army intelligence and most of his duties were top secret. His commander wasn't satisfied with Charles's unit merely accompanying the transport trucks. He wanted them to scare the rebels away with bolder methods. Over several weeks they prepared to provoke the clan's soldiers into action by increasing the amount of supplies and tempting them into attacking. Next Charles's unit began looking for

special hiding places to ambush the rebels, and the routes took them to ever more remote areas. Although strictly illegal, ambush tactics were used to set an example, contain the clan's outreach, and protect the innocent. Charles continues with his story:

> One day, we saw the clan's soldiers approach from the distance and, sure enough, they began attacking our convoy. With our long-range weapons we were able to take them out, every one of them. By the time they realized what was happening, it was too late. Mission accomplished. We then approached carefully, and turning the bodies over saw, to our horror, that many of those we had just shot were child soldiers—ten and eleven years old. For the clan the children are like serfs, virtually owned by the clan's leaders. It made me sick to realize what I had taken part in, and I was unable to talk to anyone about it for years.

Charles's self-reproach is still evident today, although he had only been obeying orders. But after twenty odd years and through living close to nature, Charles has at last found a kind of peace, or at least a cease-fire within himself.

Photo Andrew Wakeford

Jaspen Boothe

Helping homeless female veterans

Deployment: Kosovo

Served: U.S. Army

Nationality: American

Residence: Haymarket, Virginia

Occupation: Human resources officer for the Army National Guard and founder of Final Salute Inc.,
a foundation that assists homeless female veterans with housing

"God gave me a second chance at life. Now I want to repay that chance by helping others who need it most."

A beautiful woman of thirty-four overflowing with kindness and compassion for others, Jas Boothe's mission in life is to lend her talents and efforts so others can have a better life. In 2005 she was a single parent with a civilian job living in New Orleans, and she was also in the Army Reserves. "In the spring my orders came in," she says, "and I learned I would soon be deploying to Iraq."

Boothe left her civilian job, but her life was soon torn apart by two significant events. In August her personal residence received a direct hit from Hurricane Katrina. "I lost absolutely everything I ever owned in life," she recalls. "To make matters worse, I also became homeless." Boothe's life was in chaos, and then things got worse. Within weeks of the hurricane, she received a diagnosis of cancer. "I had head, neck, and throat cancer," she says, "and at that point the doctors weren't sure what my prognosis would be. It was very stressful."

Boothe's options were limited and posed some very hard choices for her. Because of her illness, the military was willing to discharge her. But Boothe needed complex full-time medical care, a job, and a place to live with her child. As long as she was receiving treatment for her cancer, she would earn full-time military pay. But as soon as that treatment ended, her health insurance and good salary would disappear. Boothe couldn't find any existing agencies or organizations that could help a homeless female veteran with a child to care for. She was stymied, but she knew she needed to stay in the military. In between radiation treatments, she flew to

Missouri to interview for a job that required her to remain in the Reserves. She finished her treatments in 2006, took the job, and moved with her son to Missouri, where they were able to live with her aunt.

Later that year, she moved to the Washington, D.C., area and returned to active duty working full time for the Army National Guard. Her cancer is in remission, but because it is an aggressive one, she will need monitoring for the rest of her life.

"My situation was very unique," says Boothe, "but I quickly realized that other female veterans also have situations that can dramatically alter their lives." In response, she created Final Salute Inc., a nonprofit agency dedicated to the needs of homeless female veterans. "We give them a boost to get on their feet," explains Boothe, who runs her foundation as a volunteer. "Our mission is to support homeless female veterans with safe and suitable housing and to assist them in other ways as needed." Boothe found a beautiful six-bedroom house in Fairfax, Virginia, and it serves as temporary housing for female veterans needing assistance.

According to Boothe, there are over 13,000 homeless female veterans in the United States. Final Salute is currently providing housing to three veterans and one child, supplying household items to two hundred, and hosting job fairs specifically for female veterans. "God gave me a second chance at life," says Boothe. "Now I want to repay that chance by helping others who need it most."

Photo Andrew Wakeford and Robert H. Miller

JORDAN DAILEY

Saving a friend's life and getting on with his own

Deployment: Iraq
Served: U. S. Army
Nationality: American
Residence: Colorado Springs, Colorado
Occupation: College student and construction worker

*"When I met Steve's family, they embraced me, immediately accepting me
as part of their family for what I'd done to protect his life."*

Jordan Dailey, twenty six, is hiding invisible scars. Many of his buddies were physically injured in combat, but he hurts on the inside. Dailey can't shake the feeling that he is responsible for his buddies' injuries, particularly those who fought under his command. But in his heart of hearts he knows he did everything he could to keep them safe. At some point, he realizes, it is the luck of the draw. Most of the injuries his buddies suffered weren't preventable, and their injuries could have just as easily been his.

His good friend from Brooklyn, Steve Femia, joined the army because his father had been in the World Trade Center on 9/11. Steve's dad made it out, but Steve felt the urge to do something after what had happened to his father. Steve and Jordan went through basic training together and were sent to Korea. The young men did not serve in the same city, and they lost touch. Jordan was promoted and sent to Iraq, and Steve ended up in his squad, one of his soldiers. The two of them were in Steve's room in Baghdad talking one day, when their base was attacked.

"Rockets and mortars and everything else were hitting our building, and AK-47 fire was going everywhere. One round hit Steve directly, it struck an artery in his neck after ricocheting off his jawbone," recalls Dailey. "It shattered his jaw." Dailey immediately applied pressure to the wound and talked his friend through it. With a medic's help, they got Steve onto a stretcher and ran as fast as they could to an aid station. Steve survived but was medically discharged from the army because of the severity of his injuries. Today he is limited in his ability to turn his neck.

Jordan visited Steve and his family afterward, and they were grateful for how he saved Steve's life. He feels a level of camaraderie with Steve that can be difficult to describe. He sometimes refers to his army buddies as his brothers, which his own brother finds confusing at times.

Returning to civilian life has been a major challenge for Jordan Dailey. Unable to sustain his relationship with his girlfriend, he began to drink too much and was issued a DUI while riding his Harley. An expensive and mortifying error, it appears to have been the wake-up call he needed to reintegrate back into normal life. Today he is taking college classes in business in the evenings and working construction during the day. Dailey hopes to combine both skills in a future career.

Photo Andrew Wakeford

GUY STERN

Distinguished professor emeritus, Wayne State University

Deployment: World War II, Europe
Served: U.S. Army
Nationality: German-American
Residence: Bloomfield Hills, Michigan
Occupation: Distinguished professor emeritus, Wayne State University,
director International Institute of the Righteous, Holocaust Memorial Center, Farmington Hills, Michigan

"We were committed to this war for personal reasons as well as ideological ones. Freedom was at stake not just in Europe but worldwide, and we worked harder, both in Camp Ritchie and in the field than anyone could have driven us. It was self-propelled energy."

Guenther Stern, eighty-nine, was born in 1922 in Hildesheim, Germany. In 1937, as a teenager, he was the only member of his family of five who was allowed to emigrate to the United States. In the following years, Stern repeatedly attempted to obtain affidavits for the rest of his family but was unsuccessful.

After high school Guenther, now called Guy, enrolled at a university, but he was inducted into the U.S. Army in 1942. After his basic training, Stern was transferred to Camp Ritchie and became a POW interrogator. Two days after D-Day Stern arrived in Normandy. Together with Fred Howard, also a Ritchie Boy, he interrogated German prisoners in France and Germany and received the Bronze Star for his "method of mass interrogation."

After Germany's capitulation Stern searched for his family, only to learn that his parents, brother, and sister had all perished in the Warsaw Ghetto. He returned to America in late 1945 to continue his studies and became an instructor for German language and literature at Columbia University, in New York. He continued his academic career at Wayne State University, in Detroit, Michigan, retiring in 2003 after thirty years there. In the early 1990s Stern had begun an association with the Holocaust Memorial Center in Farmington Hills, Michigan. When he retired from Wayne State, he became director of the Institute of the Righteous at the center.

Stern has been the recipient in both the U.S. and Germany of several distinguished awards.

Photo Robert H. Miller

James Bell

Today he is no longer homeless

Deployment: Vietnam

Served: U.S. Army

Nationality: American

Residence: Detroit, Michigan

Occupation: Employment specialist, John D. Dingell VA Medical Center

"I was known as crazy James in my neighborhood. I lived as if I was in Vietnam."

Trying to escape the streets of Detroit in the 1960s, the military seemed like a good idea for James Bell. "I tried to join the Army at sixteen," he says. "Finally, when I was seventeen they took me into basic training." At the time, Bell had no idea of the impact Vietnam was having on our society. But when told he was going to be sent there to fight, his reaction was, "Hey, I didn't sign up for this."

Arriving in Vietnam to the harsh realities of war, Bell was confronted by a near constant siege of mortars exploding around him. He was assigned to the Military Assistance Command and learned the language of the Vietcong, becoming a skillful interrogator. Bell narrowly avoided death several times by being in the right place at the wrong time. "It did not take me long to be introduced to cocaine and the benefits of being numb," he says. "On my eighteenth birthday, a fellow soldier came up to me and asked if I knew about cocaine." Bell took some of the drug from the soldier. After inhaling a big snort, he began "vomiting all over the place," he recalls.

At first Bell didn't like taking drugs, but soon the pull of wanting to fit in became a more powerful force than the drugs. "My addiction wasn't cocaine, it was heroin," he says. "I started using it regularly but refused to acknowledge I had a drug problem."

Bell's addiction spanned several years, and eventually the military was on to him. During a state-side hospitalization he became straight but relapsed after leaving on a weekend pass. James went AWOL, fleeing his unit and his responsibilities for several months. With the help of many, he returned and received an honorable discharge from the army.

"I was known as crazy James in my neighborhood," he recalls. "I lived as if I was in Vietnam. Barbed wire, booby traps laced throughout my yard, guns and pit bulls for protection. I would answer the door with a gun in my hand. At night I would dress in my combat gear and go on night operations by myself and at gunpoint stick up dope houses in and around Detroit." Taking the money and the dope gave him a big adrenaline rush and made him feel like he was in Vietnam again. "I did so many things wrong," he says. "I even fathered a child with my girlfriend back in Vietnam. To this day, I have no idea where they are in this world."

Bell had a serious heroin habit for thirty years, from 1968 to 1998. "I was eventually busted and arrested for possession but spared prison time," he explains. "The judge sentenced me to Harbor Light Rehab Center. Unfortunately, I was so out of control the physicians sent me to the VA." Bell was clean when he returned to his old neighborhood, but he soon became an addict again.

Since our original interview in April 2011, extensive counseling has helped Bell to dramatically turn his life around. "I'd had enough of my bad habits and wanted change," says Bell, who is now sixty. "I have been clean from drugs now for eleven years," he explains. While living at the Michigan Veterans Foundation homeless shelter, he heard that the job of employment specialist was opening at the John D. Dingell VA Medical Center. Bell had experience and President Obama was encouraging companies to hire homeless veterans. Bell got the job.

James Bell says he is happy, empowered, and, best of all, no longer homeless. "I'm pulling my life together, and I am real happy about it."

Photo Robert H. Miller

RICHARD LUTERMAN

Meteorological support for "Shock and Awe"

Deployment: United Arab Emirates, Operation Desert Shield
Served: U.S. Army
Nationality: American
Residence: Farmington Hills, Michigan
Occupation: Chief meteorologist, WJBK Fox 2 TV, Detroit, Michigan

*"My Operation Desert Shield experience was exciting—it was a Red, White, and Blue moment.
It had America written all over it."*

Richard Luterman, forty-five, has a great passion for life. You can see it in him as he talks. Luterman's conversation is lively, he gestures with his hands as he speaks, and a range of emotions pass over his face as he paints the picture of his life in the military.

While a student at Penn State University, Luterman's number-one interest was the weather, but he also participated in the school's ROTC program. His first ROTC assignment after graduation was as a meteorologist at an Air Force base in Upstate New York. "It wasn't long before I was deployed to serve," he recalls, "and I became part of Desert Shield. I was there about three weeks before the actual war started."

Luterman was assigned to be a weather officer attached to a small detachment; he was the officer in charge, with four other enlisted people supporting him. Together they ran an around-the-clock weather station. Luterman's job was to brief pilots as they were coming and going on combat support missions. The evening before the actual war started is one of his most vivid memories. It was January 17, 1991, and their wing commander came in and called together everyone who needed to know about the impending "Shock and Awe." As the commander spoke, it became clear to Luterman that this was going to be the real deal—America was going to war.

The commander informed the assembled group that every available plane would be leaving that night from the runway in the United Arab Emirates air base. Luterman recalls the evening:

It was a surreal moment and the tension began to rise—you could really feel it. I needed to get some rest because my shift would start in the early morning, so I returned to my hooch. I remember being awakened around 3 a.m. by tremendously loud and thunderous roaring sounds coming from the hundreds of planes taking off. I leapt out of bed and ran outside, and what I remember was my mouth being so dry and that my entire vision was filled with the intense glow in the sky from the lights on the planes leaving the runway. The planes were in line and taking off one by one. It was like a perfectly staged movie. But it wasn't a movie. It was something I was living in real life.

In the morning Luterman went to the weather station to relieve some of the exhausted men who had worked in the middle of the night to send the waves of planes aloft. He went over to the flight area and saw men and women lining the runways with American flags and banners in hand as they greeted the returning aircraft, carefully counting each one. "It was like a scene you would see in a World War II movie," recalls Luterman. "It was a Red, White, and Blue moment—it had America written all over it."

All the planes made it home safely that time, but at other times, later in the war, the euphoria would turn to sadness. "On some days planes do not come home and men and women are lost," says Luterman, "and that's the real tragedy of war." But he will never forget the pride he felt on that first night of the war. "Nothing can prepare you," he says, "for that amazing scene."

ROLAND STIGULINSZKY

Life was exciting and then it was not

Deployment: World War II, Europe
Served German Wehrmacht
Nationality: German
Residence: Saarbrucken, Germany
Occupation: Graphic designer and writer

"At the time, I was an enthusiastic member of the Hitler Youth. They were good at making it sound like a noble future was in store. Only later did we wake up to the truth behind the propaganda."

In the words of eighty-five-year-old Roland Stigulinszky:

Hitler visited Koblenz in 1934. I saw him with my uncle, who suggested I offer him my hand. I stretched my little arm toward him, but Hitler only had eyes for an old man holding a top hat, and he stood there clasping his right hand and looking into his eyes. One year later, an emigrant with dark hair was talking to my father in my mother's kitchen. I overheard the name "Hitler" a couple of times through the door and said, "I'm for Hitler, too!" This upset my father, who sent me packing. I heard my parents arguing afterward, and my mother was telling my father to keep out of it, and apart from that, he had just given the visitor the last of her household money.

In 1940 I joined the Hitler Youth. It was an exciting time and, as a result, I was able to take part in preliminary training for the Luftwaffe.

To the delight of my mother, in 1942 I went to the NPEA [the Nazi boarding school the National Political Institutes of Education]. My father was horrified, and he believed the war would be lost as soon as the Americans joined. My mother saw an international role for me in Tokyo or somewhere of importance.

So, my life was interesting and its source of inspiration was always the Fuhrer. In 1944, when I joined the Luftwaffe and flew several different types of aircraft, I thought it couldn't get much better. The day after my nineteenth birthday, the Berlin Radio announced that Hitler had fallen. On May 8, 1945, I crossed the River Elbe as an infantry soldier and was again confronted by the Americans. They sent me back to the Russians, who kept me as a prisoner until 1947, when I was sent home suffering from malnutrition.

Photo Andrew Wakeford

Each veteran has a story

TONY VACCARO

Pouring chemicals into helmets and developing photos in foxholes

Deployment: World War II, Europe

Served: U.S. Army

Nationality: American

Residence: Long Island City, New York

Occupation: Professional photographer

"My approach to taking combat pictures was simple. No matter what, if my eye sees it—take the picture."

At age ninety Tony Vaccaro remains a truly amazing man. His astonishing achievements, first as a World War II combat photographer, and then as a lead photographer for the iconic American magazines *Life*, *Look*, and *Flair*, have set him apart from others in his field. In his Long Island City, New York, flat on a hot July day photos of the famous peer down from the walls—Sophia Loren, Georgia O'Keeffe, Frank Lloyd Wright—and are stacked in every corner of the room. "I have photographed almost every famous person who was deemed newsworthy over the last fifty years," says Vaccaro.

Vaccaro began his career as a photographer when he was drafted into the Army in 1943. He served in the 83rd Infantry Division and fought in 1944 and 1945 as a private in Normandy and Germany. The Army quickly discovered he could speak Italian, French, and German and that he had extensive experience developing photos. His superiors handed him an M1 rifle and an Argus C3 camera, and his life as a combat photographer began. "I have seen so much human trauma," he says, "it's amazing I have not went crazy." Vaccaro took nearly ten-thousand photographs during World War II. What is more amazing is how many rolls of film he developed on the field of battle. Vaccaro shares this story:

> I was pretty naïve when I first started. I was in Normandy and the battles were going on all around me. I had about ten rolls of film that needed developing. Thinking to myself that every village has a camera store or newspaper office where I could find a darkroom to develop my film, I quickly realized the entire area of Normandy was in shambles. Every city and its buildings were destroyed to rubble. What was I going to do?

Vaccaro was stumped. As the battles raged around him, he made his way through the rubble and unexpectedly encountered a wall still standing with an AGFA Photographic sign barely clinging to it. Sifting through the building's remains, Vaccaro was amazed to find the darkroom chemicals he needed to develop his film.

> I immediately lugged three glass bottles back to our camp. Later that night I persuaded my three friends to loan me their helmets. They thought I was a little crazy. After dark I stood in my foxhole and lined up the helmets, mixing up the chemicals and filling each helmet. I developed each roll by keeping a portion of it inside the chemical and alternating my raised arms up and down so that the entire length of film was saturated with the chemical. I repeated this for the developer, stop bath, and hypo. The final helmet held water and was used to wash off the chemicals. I hung each roll of developed film from branches of a tree to dry overnight. The next morning I rolled them all together and placed them inside a film can and sent them on their way.

Firing a rifle with one hand and taking a picture with the other often put Vaccaro in harm's way. He was slightly wounded–grazed by a bullet—while shooting a photo and was awarded a Purple Heart. Vaccaro's skillful eye and abundant courage resulted in one of the most complete visual records of World War II in existence. Today he continues to shoot photos and work in his darkroom developing them. It is what he enjoys most.

Photo Robert H. Miller

THERESE COONEY

Becoming a better and more courageous person while coping with PTSD

Deployment: Stateside
Served: U.S. Army
Nationality: American
Residence: Oak Park, Michigan
Occupation: Disabled surgical technologist

Cooney experienced what every member of the armed services dreads: the death of a fellow soldier standing right beside her.

Therese Cooney, forty-eight, is wearing a sleeveless T-shirt and the tattoo on her right arm is plainly visible. Cooney looks like someone who cannot be easily pushed around. Stoic and very serious, she occasionally breaks into a smile that reveals a softer side. "Before I joined the army I was a private airplane pilot. My dream was to fly helicopters in the army," she says. "I joined the Army in 1982 and served until 1987 to fulfill that dream for me."

Unfortunately, Cooney's dream was shattered by two training accidents that have scarred her forever. A routine combat exercise resulted in a charge prematurely exploding, damaging her eyes and temporarily taking her vision away. Within a week Cooney was well enough to return to combat training exercises, but the explosion had marred her emotionally. "I had some vision loss but could continue with my service," she says. Constantly on edge and now afraid of any loud noise or explosion, Cooney suppressed her fears and pushed on.

Right before Cooney's training was to end, the unthinkable happened. She experienced what every member of the armed services dreads: the death of a fellow soldier standing right beside her. Cooney and a friend, also a woman, were in a foxhole next to a firing range. "My friend clicked the safety latch on her M-16, setting it into the automatic position, and leaned the gun against the dirt wall inside the foxhole, just as we were trained to do," recalls Cooney. "With her hand still on the barrel, it started continuously firing, pumping so many bullets in her within one second that there was nothing anyone could do." Cooney tried to pull her friend away from the stream of bullets, but she was already dead. "To this very day," says Cooney, "I still believe I could have done more to save her—I am just loaded with guilt."

After the service, Cooney wanted a change and became a surgical technologist. Her PTSD worsened and began to simmer inside of her. No longer able to cope with her memories, ordinary events became overwhelming and crushing, pushing her into despair. In 2005 Cooney went on disability. She is being counseled for her PTSD at the John D. Dingell VA Hospital in Detroit, where she is making positive strides.

Cooney says that the army did a lot for her, helping her to become a better and more courageous person. "It also offered me a chance to serve my country," she says. "There is always some good present, even in a terrible situation. I just hope my PTSD will eventually subside, but now I am disabled and spend my time trying to get well."

Photo Robert H. Miller

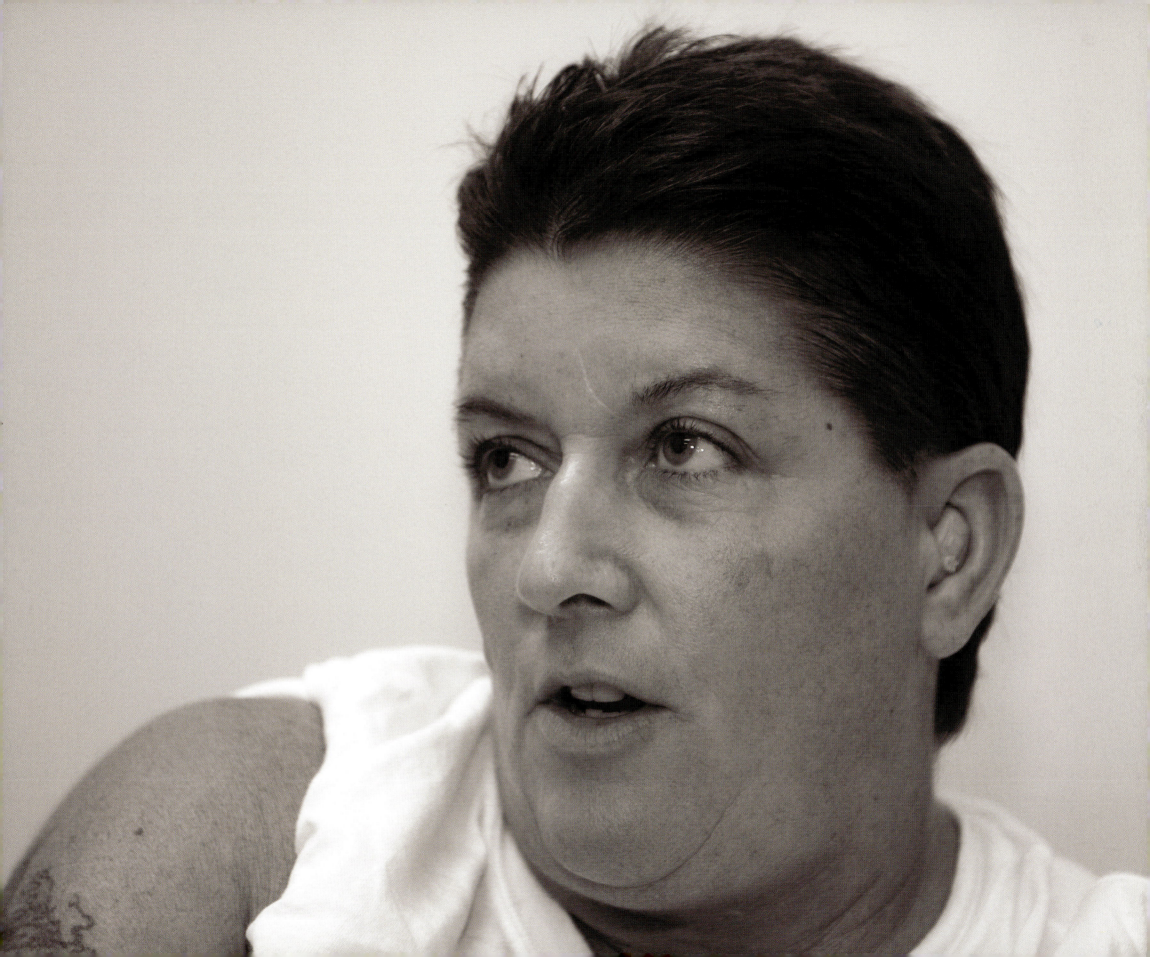

JOSEPH MAXWELL CLELAND

Disabled veteran and former U.S. senator

Deployment: Vietnam
Served: U.S. Army
Nationality: American
Residence: Washington D.C.
Occupation: Former U.S. senator and
secretary of the American Battle Monuments Commission

"Being a soldier, fighting for this country, is neither Republican nor Democrat."

On April 8, 1968 with a month left in his tour, Max Cleland was ordered to set up a radio relay station on a nearby hill. A helicopter flew him and two soldiers to the treeless top of Hill 471, east of Khe Sanh. Cleland knew some of the soldiers camped there from Operation Pegasus. He told the pilot he was going to stay a while with friends. When the helicopter landed, Cleland jumped out, followed by the two soldiers.

They ducked beneath the rotors and turned to watch the liftoff. Cleland reached down to pick up a grenade he believed had popped off his flak jacket. It exploded, and the blast slammed him backward, shredding both his legs and one arm. Due to the severity of his injuries, doctors amputated both of Cleland's legs above the knee and his right forearm. Now sixty-nine, Cleland was twenty-five at the time he was injured.

Photo Andrew Wakeford

FRANK TOWERS

Atrocities of war

Deployment: World War II, Europe
Served: U.S. Army
Nationality: American
Residence: Brooker, Florida
Occupation: Farmer, specializing in the chicken business (retired)

"I often wonder what this world would be like if those six million had never perished."

In early April 1945, the 30th Infantry Division liberated Brunswick and was headed to Magdeburg. "We found something else they weren't prepared for," Frank Towers, ninety-four, recalls. It was an idling train crammed with about 2,500 Jews. The cars, which were meant to hold about forty people, each held as many as one hundred. They were so crowded, he said, that it was impossible for everyone to get to the sole bucket in the corner, which was the bathroom. "There was a horrendous stench," says Towers. "It was so bad our own American boys had to turn around and vomit."

FRANK W. TOWERS JR.

Sadly, the Vietnam War was not a popular one

Deployment: Vietnam

Served: U.S. Army

Nationality: American

Residence: Newberry, Florida

Occupation: Retired Federal Mogul sales executive

*"War leads to bonds of friendship unlike any other bonds you will ever create.
After being in the Vietnam jungle for ninety days straight, those bonds become part of your DNA."*

Frank Towers Jr. is stoic and proud. Fit and trim, the sixty-one-year-old appears far younger than his age. Towers recalls the emotions and fears he experienced during the Vietnam War and the deaths he witnessed there as if they happened yesterday.

Remembering his war, Towers turns serious and begins to speak with candor. "The most vivid and hardest memory for me is of when I left the states for Vietnam," he says. "For me it was pretty emotional and scary." He continues:

> I had no idea what to expect, I didn't understand the war nor could I grasp the overwhelming feeling of uncertainly that war brings. Everything in my life was turned upside down. Adding to this, the Vietnam culture was so incredibly different—it was a total culture shock for me. When we landed, I was immediately placed in an infantry unit and we all moved into the belly of the jungle to fight for ninety days. Spending three months in a jungle is a miserable experience. While I was out there I contracted malaria and became violently sick after drinking stagnant water out of a bomb crater in order to survive. I finally recovered, but this took a huge toll on my body. As the war proceeded, fighting was almost constant. I was hit by shrapnel but recovered pretty quickly. I lost several of my very best buddies out there, and that forever changed me. I missed

those guys, but life in the jungle went on. I did my job and managed to survive and eventually return to the U.S., which was one of the happiest times of my life.

Once Frank Jr. was back from his tour of duty, his father, World War II vet Frank Towers, understood what his son had experienced. "My father was a great support for me," recalls Towers. "Sadly the Vietnam War was not a popular one, and we were treated very differently than the veterans returning home from World War II." According to Towers, it was hard to be a veteran back from Vietnam living in the United States at that time. "Nobody cared—nobody asked what it was like to serve or to be over there," he says. "Some people actually went out of their way to mistreat you. It was really a sad time in America."

Towers and his father share the experience of serving in a war. Both men received Purple Hearts for injuries they sustained while fighting. But Towers's father returned to an America that was greeting soldiers with ticker-tape parades and praising them for their service and accomplishments. When Frank Jr. returned to America, he was expected to slip quietly back into society and immediately function normally.

But father and son are equally proud of having served their country in a time of war.

RUDOLF STRASSNER

POW Russia

Deployment: World War II, Europe
Served: German Wehrmacht
Nationality: German
Residence: Saarbruecken, Germany
Occupation: Pianist and composer

"They took us straight from school to the Volkssturm. *We had no idea how to fight."*

Rudi Strassner sits reflecting on his war experiences, shaking his head at the unlikelihood of it all. "We were in the finishing stages of our *abitur* [high school diploma], when it was decided we were needed for the war effort," recalls Strassner. "The Volkssturm [Hitler's desperate attempt to create a new 'people's army' near the end of the war] took boys as young as sixteen and men as old as sixty. We were dispatched to Czechoslovakia to work as flak helpers in an anti-aircraft unit." It was the final months of World War II, and after a short time the unit was captured by the Russians and taken to a prisoner-of-war camp in the town of Brjansk-Beshiza, about two hundred kilometers south of Moscow. Rudi was one of eleven thousand inmates at the camp.

On entering the mess hall, he noticed a grand piano—he was already a very keen pianist—so he immediately sat down and began to play Bach and some of his own compositions. The camp commander, quite a formidable woman, took note and talked to him about his capabilities. Strassner was then only seventeen, but he was immediately assigned the duty of starting up an orchestra in the camp.

Strassner managed to get his hands on some instruments for other willing inmates to play and was soon writing scores for each participant.

In no time he was given other privileges, like offering piano lessons to people from the local community and being allowed to leave the camp to order sheet music for concerts. His imprisonment in Russia was in complete contrast to the suffering that others had to endure. Rudi's only work assignment in the labor camp was to advance his musical agenda.

After four years in Russia Strassner was finally released, in 1949, to go home to Germany. He was delighted, of course, and feeling happy and grateful to have avoided being sent to Siberia. But he knew well that only his talents as a composer and performer had kept him in a position of privilege.

Today, at eighty-three, Rudi Strassner is still composing. He has often thought about the Russians' legendary love of music and the role that music can play in encouraging peace. Strassner tells the story of his POW experience with an embarrassed expression, remembering the fate of others not so lucky. Yet the humanity he expressed through his artistry, he believes, enabled him to thrive in the camp and be appreciated by his fellow inmates and members of the surrounding community. After the trauma of being in a war, music had inspired the strong and positive connections he forged with his former enemies.

Photo Andrew Wakeford

BRETT FELTON

Disabled veteran

Deployment: Iraq War
Served: U.S. Army
Nationality: Polish American
Residence: Warren, Michigan
Occupation: Logistics engineer, General Dynamics Land Systems

"The Iraq War made me numb, almost lifeless."

Brett Felton, twenty-four, is wearing a Rosary around his neck and a religious bracelet on his left wrist as he sits in his Warren, Michigan, home talking about his experiences in the Iraq War. Felton stares into space, his eyes wide and almost lifeless, as he describes his fifteen months in hell and explains how he survived an IED attack (improvised explosion device). He paints a surreal picture in painstaking detail. While Felton doesn't appear disabled, the body under his clothes and the memories that lodge deep inside his mind tell a completely different story.

"The Iraq War made me numb, almost lifeless." says Felton. "I arrived in July 2006, and from that day forward my world was filled with uncertainty and death." Felton's eyes tear up as he recalls how much he hated all the killing going on around him. "But it was either them or me," he says. "When I came to Iraq I was determined to survive."

Although Felton wasn't afraid to die, he says he was anxious most of the time. But the "costs" of war significantly changed his attitude and physical life. Today the Veterans Administration classifies Brett Felton as 70 percent disabled. Felton relives the deadly IED explosion that almost took his life:

I was a CROWS gunner in a Humvee for route patrol. Insurgents target this first if they plan on an attack. I knew this position was a very dangerous one. My job was surveillance, and I had the gun and the high power scopes with night vision to find and defend against them if necessary. I was inside the Humvee with two other soldiers. We relied on each other. It happened when we were nearing the end of an intense fourteen-hour patrol. Some insurgent most likely triggered the IED by a cell phone right when

our Humvee was passing over it. We never saw a thing.

Felton saw the explosion before he heard it. It seemed to happen in slow motion. "A thick black cloud of dust and smoke appeared, and in an instant it engulfed us," he says. "I have never experienced anything like this–super black and intense. I was choking."

For a moment the explosion consumed all the surrounding breathable air, with the soldiers taking in dust, smoke, and sand. Soon Felton's ears were popping, and he could hear an intense painful ringing. "Within seconds I lost all of my hearing," he recalls. After that he fell unconscious, and when he came to, his first thought was: This is forever. "I thought I was dead," he says. It took several minutes for Felton to process what had happened to him. Realizing he could still hear sounds above the intense ringing in his ears, he became aware of the frantic screaming of his injured truck commander. "Is everyone OK? Is everyone OK?" the team leader was shouting. At this moment Felton understood he was not dead and that the pain in his body was escalating.

Occasionally a hint of sunlight glinted through the thick, dark smoke. The Humvee was destroyed, but the men inside had survived–barely. Felton had suffered a closed-head injury, spinal compression, and several other disabling injuries. The others had taken in shrapnel from flying IED and Humvee debris, and all had suffered compression injuries and blunt-force trauma. The injuries inflicted on Felton and his fellow soldiers in that attack endure today and have changed all of their lives forever.

"It's not always the shrapnel that kills the soldier, but the percussion from the blast," says Felton. "We were just damn lucky."

Photo Robert H. Miller

RUTH (HEIDI) HYDE-COLE

Playing games with Allied soldiers

Deployment: World War II, England

Served: The Red Cross

Nationality: American

Residence: Queensbury, New York

Occupation: Homemaker, nursery school educator, and professional Girl Scout coordinator (retired)

"There were so many men who desperately needed attention and someone to talk to."

Heidi Hyde-Cole, ninety-one, wears her original Red Cross pin on the right lapel of her coat. She is very proud of her service with the international humanitarian organization in England during World War II.

Warm, friendly, and witty, Hyde-Cole still exhibits the passion and drive that sustained her when she took on that war assignment sixty-seven years ago. "I wear my pin every day," she says, "and I am so glad I had the chance to serve." Hyde-Cole says her job description back then was simple: "I was to play games with the Allied soldiers." Games soon turned into discussions. "There were so many men who desperately needed attention and someone to talk to," she recalls. "Any diversion from that horrible war was a welcome relief for them. Most of the soldiers were scared to death to return to the front lines of fighting."

Hyde-Cole remembers the plight of one soldier in particular: "This poor man was covered with burns from his head to his toes. He had white bandages wrapped around him, and the only openings were his eyes, mouth and ears." He still managed to smile, she remembers, but she knew his pain and suffering were intense. "At first this soldier wanted nothing to do with a recreation director," she says, "because it reminded him too much of home." But soon, she says, "he warmed up to me and benefited from being diverted from the thoughts of his injuries."

Hyde-Cole remembers her Red Cross experience as an adventure. She decided to volunteer because she wasn't married and wanted to do whatever she could to support the war effort. "One of the scariest parts was coming over to England on the Queen Mary," says Hyde-Cole. "The Germans submarines laid a target on any boat that was crossing the Atlantic." All the ships were zig-zagging their way across the ocean, she says, and, fortunately, "the Queen Mary was built for speed and needed no escort. I remember falling out of bed late one night on one quick zag. Or was it a zig? We eventually arrived safely in England." She also remembers an English waiter in the dining room of the ship. "He was an interesting fellow," says Hyde-Cole. "I finally got up the nerve to ask him if he had a girlfriend. He told me, 'Oh, no. I have a little bit of fluff in every port.'"

For the first time in her life, Heidi Hyde-Cole was speechless.

Photo Robert H. Miller

ROGER DIEDERICH

Tough adventures and a lot of luck

Deployment: World War II, Europe
Served: Forced recruit in the German Wehrmacht
Nationality: Luxembourg
Residence: Contern, Luxembourg
Occupation: Technical office manager (retired)

"On my way home, I had four different nationalities."

Roger Diederich, eighty-two, is an alert man whose past experiences are still very much a part of his life. "No one wanted to work for the Germans when they invaded Luxembourg in 1940," he recalls. "They came and told us that Luxembourg was now German." In 1942 the resistance in Luxembourg was considerable, and it was the only country where workers went on strike in protest of the occupation. The Germans executed twenty-one of those strikers.

Young men born in 1929, including Diederich, were soon sent to work in forced labor or made to join the German Army. "Most of us thought that labor would be less dangerous," says Diederich, "so like many of my friends I chose labor over being a soldier in the Wehrmacht." He was hoping to escape while on leave and join the underground movement. But Diederich was in Poland when the Americans liberated Luxembourg, and after that no one was allowed any leave time.

The Germans now promoted the joys of becoming Wehrmacht soldiers to their Luxembourg workers. They even dangled membership in the SS before them. "They said to us, 'You can speak out, you are among friends,'" recalls Diederich. But the entire Luxembourg contingent remained unimpressed, and not one of them volunteered. Unfortunately, three or four Luxembourgers spoke out and said they would desert to the other side if forced to the German front. According to Diederich, they were sent to concentration camps and shot.

Diederich became a most reluctant member of the Wehrmacht, and he remembers many deserting in Slonsk, Poland. Those caught trying to make it to the underground were dealt with mercilessly. On one night alone ninety-one were executed. Others were sent to the Eastern Front, which was an incredibly dangerous fate. There were eight Luxembourgers in Diederich's company who managed to maintain careful communication and look after one another. Working as a radio operator, Diederich was only fifty yards away from the Russian front. Somehow he survived the war without injury.

After the war ended, Diederich and his fellow Luxembourgers were left to make their way home on foot. In Chemnitz, in Occupied Germany, American trucks transported them westward. Placed in a camp for a while, he became part of a French group; at the next camp, he was told that Belgians were being transported home. He didn't have any papers but was accepted as a Belgian. Soon he learned that a group from Holland was at the next camp and about to be on its way. Although he did not speak Dutch, he managed to find a spot on their train home. Then he discovered it was actually headed to a prison. But luckily the train was diverted to Luxembourg. Diederich jumped out and made his way home, finally reclaiming his real nationality.

Photo Andrew Wakeford

CHRISTOPHER EDWARDS

A shortcut leads to wounds that time does not heal

Deployment: Iraq
Served: U.S. Army
Nationality: American
Residence: Jacksonville, Florida
Occupation: Career military

"My ten-year-old son doesn't know me any way but hurt. He was too young when it happened to have remembered me."

Christopher Edwards is forty years old and a survivor of a 2005 roadside bomb from the war in Iraq. He was in a Bradley fighting vehicle on a route-clearing mission in a small town called Usufia, south of Baghdad, and in command of the five soldiers traveling with him. They had taken a shorter route back to the base when they ran into the bomb, which had been detonated by a cell-phone signal. Luckily, the mortars were pointing sideways instead of upwards, so much of the four-hundred-pound blast was channeled out instead of up. But the entire crew of six was injured, though none quite as badly as their commander.

Edwards suffered burns over 80 percent of his body and was hospitalized for nine months. He spent five of those months in an induced coma in an intensive care unit at San Antonio Medical Center. He has had over 120 surgeries, including many skin grafts. Because of traumatic brain injuries, he also had some cognitive difficulties. But today his speech is fine and his sense of humor intact, and he says he feels glad to be alive given that his chances of survival, in retrospect, had been fairly slim. His use of his hands and legs is severely limited, but he manages with the help of his army buddies to get around and is still in active service.

Edwards remembers the attack in vivid detail, and in the early weeks after he was injured, before he was put in a medically-induced coma, he had dreams about it every night. But his memories of that day have helped him come to terms with the attack. He had been tired, hot, hungry, and thirsty and he'd been up for thirty-six hours. It was his decision to take the shorter route that drastically changed the lives of six people and their families. Of course, the longer journey might have proved equally dangerous.

Edwards is the father of three boys, ages ten, fifteen, and eighteen. His relationship with them has changed since the attack:

> My ten-year-old son doesn't know me any way but hurt. He was too young when it happened to remember me, and now he is growing up much more quickly than a ten year old should. My other boys don't know me the way they used to because I have changed so much. My wife went from being a wife to being a nurse and a caregiver overnight. I feel a lot of guilt and indulge in some second guessing sometimes, when I think about these things.

The claim that time heals all wounds, says Edwards, isn't true.

BRIAN RATZLAFF

F4 jet pilot and POW at the Hanoi Hilton

Deployment: Vietnam

Served: U.S. Air Force

Nationality: American

Residence: Davisburg Michigan

Occupation: Northwest Airlines pilot (retired)

"I knew the war was over for good when I saw CBS News anchor Walter Cronkite walk into our camp."

Brian Ratzlaff, sixty-eight, is taking every opportunity to insert a smile or a joke as he recalls his last moments flying his F4 jet during the Vietnam War. Suddenly his conversation turns serious as he describes his plane taking a direct hit. "The missile came out of nowhere," he recalls, "and just knocked the tail off from my plane and immediately set fire to my missiles." He remembers his back-seat man (co-pilot) saying, "If we get one more flashing light on this instrument panel, we're going to get a free game!" Within seconds the fast-moving, non-responsive F4 jet had twisted and rolled upside down, its nose pointing slightly downward as it began its death plunge into the fields far below.

"The first thing I thought was I was mad as hell for taking a hit," says Ratzlaff, "that's what fighter pilots do—we take things like this very seriously." Realizing he was in a no-win situation, he decided to punch out and eject. "It seemed like twenty minutes before it was my turn," he recalls. Fortunately, when he was finally able to eject, everything happened on schedule and, within seconds, after a monstrous explosion, he felt G-forces pushing him into his seat as the rocket thrust beneath him hurled him away from the cockpit. "I believe we ejected at well over four hundred knots," Ratzlaff says (in layman terms, that is almost five hundred miles per hour). "You get pretty beat up at those speeds, even sitting in an ejection seat.

"The war was going on as we were coming down. There was a lot of shooting and bombing. Looking up from my seat, I discovered my parachute had holes in it," says Ratzlaff. "To this day, I'm not sure if it was from ejecting so fast or if I caught some rounds as I was coming down." He landed in thick bamboo, cut himself loose, and found a place to hide. Ratzlaff spent two days alone under the vines and bushes. North Vietnamese soldiers were as close as five feet away, but he managed to remain undetected. "They knew I was there, because my parachute was at the bottom of the hill," he recalls. Eventually he needed to look for food and water and stepped over a log, right on top of a sleeping North Vietnamese soldier. "That was it, I was captured."

Ratzlaff went by jeep to Hanoi, where he became a POW at what American soldiers referred to as the "Hanoi Hilton." Ratzlaff spent a month in solitary confinement under round-the-clock interrogation. After that, he was put with other Americans. "I was constantly being threatened with being shot, but it did not take long for me to figure out it was only bluffs," he says. "As long as I did what they asked, it seemed I would be OK."

With the war escalating, President Nixon ordered extensive bombing. "This shook the hell out of me and everyone else—it was never-ending," recalls Ratzlaff. Finally, after nine months in captivity, he and his fellow POWs heard the war was ending, and they were abruptly transferred to another camp.

"I knew the war was over for good," says Ratzlaff, "when I saw CBS News anchor Walter Cronkite walk into our camp."

HELEN ROSARIO

Getting shot at was an everyday occurrence

Deployment: Iraq and Afghanistan
Served: U.S. Army
Nationality: American
Residence: Colorado Springs, Colorado
Occupation: Martial arts teacher, LifeQuest Transitions

"We are the first line of medical care, and sometimes we are the last."

As an army medic Helen Rosario was frequently in as much danger as the combat soldiers, and getting shot at became an everyday occurrence for her. "You'd go out, maybe get shot at, maybe not," she says. "Maybe we'd watch the road in front of us get blown up twenty feet in the air, maybe not. Maybe you'd need to change a tire while a battle was going on, maybe not. Here in the U.S. people freak out over a pothole in the road or about what they'll have for dinner."

The science of the past few years has advanced in leaps and bounds, according to the young and energetic Rosario, who is twenty-five. She explains that centers for traumatic brain injuries are being set up all over the U.S. and all sorts of subtleties unknown or little understood during previous conflicts are being discovered. In past wars, as often as not, concussion was diagnosed after a bomb blast, and the patient was simply advised to avoid falling asleep for the next forty-eight hours. Now modern technology allows medical professionals to quickly learn which areas of the brain have suffered the most damage. But back in 2003, when the army entered Fallujah, none of this was known, says Rosario.

In September 2009, returning from a supply mission in the Nangahar province to their base in Jalalabad, Rosario and others in their truck noticed all the lights were out in the area and there weren't any cars on the streets. Suddenly they were hit by four armor-piercing RPGs. Because they were traveling at fifty-five miles per hour, their truck quickly passed through the line of fire. But the driver lost his left leg above the knee and Rosario suffered severe internal burns and other injuries to her head. At first she couldn't see or breathe. But as soon as Rosario was able, she applied a tourniquet to her driver's wounds and provided cover fire. Because of her concern for the driver, she initially had been unaware of her own injuries.

Rosario later had brain surgery for a ruptured cyst, which had temporarily blinded her. Her hearing had also been badly damaged in the attack. She was awarded a bronze star for valor in April 2010, but her doctors would not allow her to return to combat. She says she has no regrets, because her driver survived, but she frequently relives the horrors of that night in her dreams.

Today she teaches martial arts at LifeQuest Transitions, a nonprofit organization that serves wounded soldiers.

Photo Andrew Wakeford

IN WAR, THERE ARE NO UNWOUNDED SOLDIERS.

— Jose Narosky

FRANCIS LIVSEY

Blown off a ship in the Battle of Okinawa

Deployment: World War II, Pacific
Served: U.S. Navy
Nationality: American
Residence: Midland, Michigan
Occupation: Retired insurance executive

"I can still see the kamikaze pilot tipping his wings vertical in his effort to have maximum speed for impact on our ship."

With his smiling eyes and warm smile Francis Livsey, eighty-seven, is proud of his experiences in the Navy during World War II. After graduating from high school, Livsey wanted to enlist in the Air Corps. He passed all the required tests but the vision one. "I flunked because I could not hold both eyes on a white ruler," he recalls. Refusing to be deterred, Livsey went down the street to the next recruitment office and joined the Navy.

A natural leader and with the smarts to go with it, Livsey quickly excelled in the Navy. His commander immediately promoted him and wanted to send him to Alaska on a special assignment. But Livsey didn't want to go to Alaska. "I want to be on board a ship, I want to sail on the oceans," Livsey recalls telling the commander.

Soon he was assigned to the USS Sangamon and bound for the Pacific war. Arriving near the island of Okinawa in May 1945, the USS Sangamon joined a large flotilla of ships about to engage with the Japanese. The Battle of Okinawa was ruthless and dangerous. Japanese bombers followed by kamikaze pilots, their planes loaded with explosives, were taking aim against the American ships fighting in the China Sea. Livsey recalls that day:

It was just awful. Soon there were twenty-four kamikaze pilots reported in the area all taking aim at various ships in an effort to destroy them. I was working near a 40 mm gun that was firing away, when the first kamikaze plane locked in and took aim at our ship. Fortunately he missed my area by twenty-five feet and crashed into the sea. Within seconds, another one had locked its aim at us and hit us near mid-ship. I can still see the plane's wings tipped vertically so he could get maximum speed for impact—and the kill.

Livsey's only memory of the moment the plane hit was of first seeing and then feeling an all-encompassing orange explosion and being blown off the deck into the sea. "It's a long way down to the water from the flight deck," he recalls. Coming up for air, Livsey found holes in his life jacket and couldn't get it to inflate. He ditched the jacket and, amazingly, without a scratch on his body, started to swim away from the ship. "So there I was in the water," he says, "my ship was burning from end to end, and no land in sight—what was I going to do?"

Livsey remained calm, soon noticing a wooden table from the ship's mess hall floating nearby. He swam over to it and grabbed on and then began hollering at two other men struggling in the water. Livsey and the two men were in the water for about six hours before being picked up by the USS Dennis. While floating in the China Sea they had enjoyed a front-row seat for the remainder of the battle.

The Japanese air strike against the Sangamon resulted in eleven dead, twenty-five missing, and twenty-one seriously injured. Once the fire was put out, the Sangamon was able to sail back to port for extensive repairs. "I know I was a lucky man," says Livsey, "but in reality I tried not to think or worry about anything at the time. I'm just glad I wasn't killed that day."

Photo Robert H. Miller

Mona Lisa Sarin

Recovering from PTSD and restarting a life

Deployment: Iraq War, Hawaii

Served: U.S. Army

Nationality: American

Residence: Washington, D.C.

Occupation: Homeless

"Sometimes the most painful wounds are the ones you can't see."

You would never know Mona Lisa Sarin, fifty-one, is a homeless veteran. Always smiling and articulate, Sarin tries to remain positive in face of the horrible things that happened to her while in the Army. Sarin joined in 1998 with the intent of making it her career. "I had all the best intentions," she says. "I was thrilled to be stationed in Hawaii, where I could start to live my dream."

Unfortunately Sarin's dream of a military career was shattered soon after she arrived in Hawaii. "Sometimes the most painful wounds are the ones you can't see," says Sarin. What she is referring to is the verbal, physical, and sexual abuse she experienced from her commanding sergeant. "His intention was to get me alone during a spontaneous inspection of my barracks," she recalls. "With no one around, he quickly became a monster and pressed me for sex." Sarin refused his advances and that's when it turned ugly. He became violent and abusive, and she could smell the alcohol on his breath. "I fought back hard and there was blood on both sides," recalls Sarin. She finally escaped and immediately sought help from her senior commanding general. The Army started an investigation that would last several months, and that is when Sarin's military career turned south. When the news filtered through the ranks, she says she instantly became "the bad guy." Before long she was receiving daily threats and that escalated into full-scale physical abuse. "Everybody loved this sergeant and thought he was a stellar individual," she says. A few others she knew understood he had a dark side, but everyone else thought she was trying to destroy his career.

Things became so dangerous for Sarin that before the trial she was shot at during training exercises and cornered inside an elevator and beat up. But Sarin would not back down. After a long investigation and trial, the sergeant was found guilty, sentenced, and demoted. For her personal protection, Sarin was transferred to San Francisco to finish out her military career.

Eventually returning to civilian life, Sarin tried to act like nothing was wrong. But Post-Traumatic Stress Disorder took control of her, and the rigors of work and life became too much to bear. With her life spiraling down, Sarin sought the help of the VA.

Sarin's official diagnosis is Post Traumatic Stress Disorder–Military Sexual Trauma (PTSD/MST). Because of her illness and the depression that comes with it, Sarin couldn't work. She lost her job and was evicted from her apartment. With no family to fall back on, Sarin joined the ranks of the homeless.

Her home state of Georgia had nothing to offer her, so Sarin found help from Final Salute Inc., a nonprofit organization in Washington, D.C., dedicated to helping female homeless veterans. She was offered a room in a house and money to travel to Washington, and she is now in the process of putting her life back on track.

Sarin lives with six other homeless female veterans, and today she is the "big sister" of the house. Sarin is one of an estimated 11,000 homeless female veterans in the United States. She is receiving extensive therapy and looks forward to regaining her independent life and restarting her career.

Photo Andrew Wakeford and Robert H. Miller

DAVID OESCHGER

The mysterious workings of General Patton

Deployment: Iraq (twice), Afghanistan, Kosovo, Macedonia, Bosnia
Served: U.S. Army
Nationality: American
Residence: Baumholder, Germany
Occupation: Battalion commander

"We entered a building as two suicide bombers blew themselves up, and it collapsed around me.
I had five pelvic fractures, five broken ribs, a punctured lung, and extensive internal damage."

David Oeschger, forty-four, looks fighting fit, and it is difficult to believe he is recovering from serious injuries. A thousand soldiers were under his command in Arusgan, Afghanistan, and it gives him great satisfaction to know they worked (and still work) very well together mentoring the local police and collaborating with Australian soldiers. But all were well aware of the danger when, in late summer 2011, the Taliban began to advance toward their town.

One day his unit learned that suicide bombers from Pakistan were approaching. Oeschger describes the scene after the bombs were detonated:

> The Taliban gained no advantage, there were no civilian casualties, and none of my soldiers died. First, explosions occurred and suicide bombers were sent to blow themselves up in front of the gates of official Afghanistan government areas. We reacted quickly. I had patrols ready to go out the gate, and we were immediately engaged in a firefight. Over the course of three hours, with the use of about fifteen vehicles, forty-five soldiers, and air weapons teams, we engaged and destroyed two suicide bombers and their support elements. Unfortunately, we entered a building as two suicide bombers blew themselves up, and it collapsed around me. I had five pelvic fractures, five broken ribs, a punctured lung, and extensive internal damage.

Oeschger attributes his extraordinary recovery to the wonderful support he has received from his family: his wife, Jennifer, and their two daughters, Jacqueline and Sophia. He has been through reconstructive surgery in Landstuhl Hospital, in Germany, and at the new Walter Reed Army Medical Center, in Bethesda, Maryland, and he says the care and advanced medical technology have helped him to quickly get back on his feet.

Oeschger regrets that he can no longer command his soldiers. But he knows that while he is recovering a number of them are returning to the U.S., and he intends to reconnect with many of his finest. After twenty-two years in the Army, he hopes that, despite his injuries, he will be able to continue his career in the military.

Jennifer Oeschger tells the story of her family visiting General George Patton's grave in Hamm Cemetery, in Luxembourg, in 2010. Their oldest daughter, Jacqueline, who at the time was eleven, wrote Patton a letter and left it on his grave, asking the general to look after her dad, who was about to deploy to Afghanistan.

David Oeschger, once badly injured, no longer takes any medications and is now on his way to a complete recovery. Perhaps General Patton, always concerned for the welfare of the troops on the battlefield, had a hand in this outcome.

Photo Andrew Wakeford

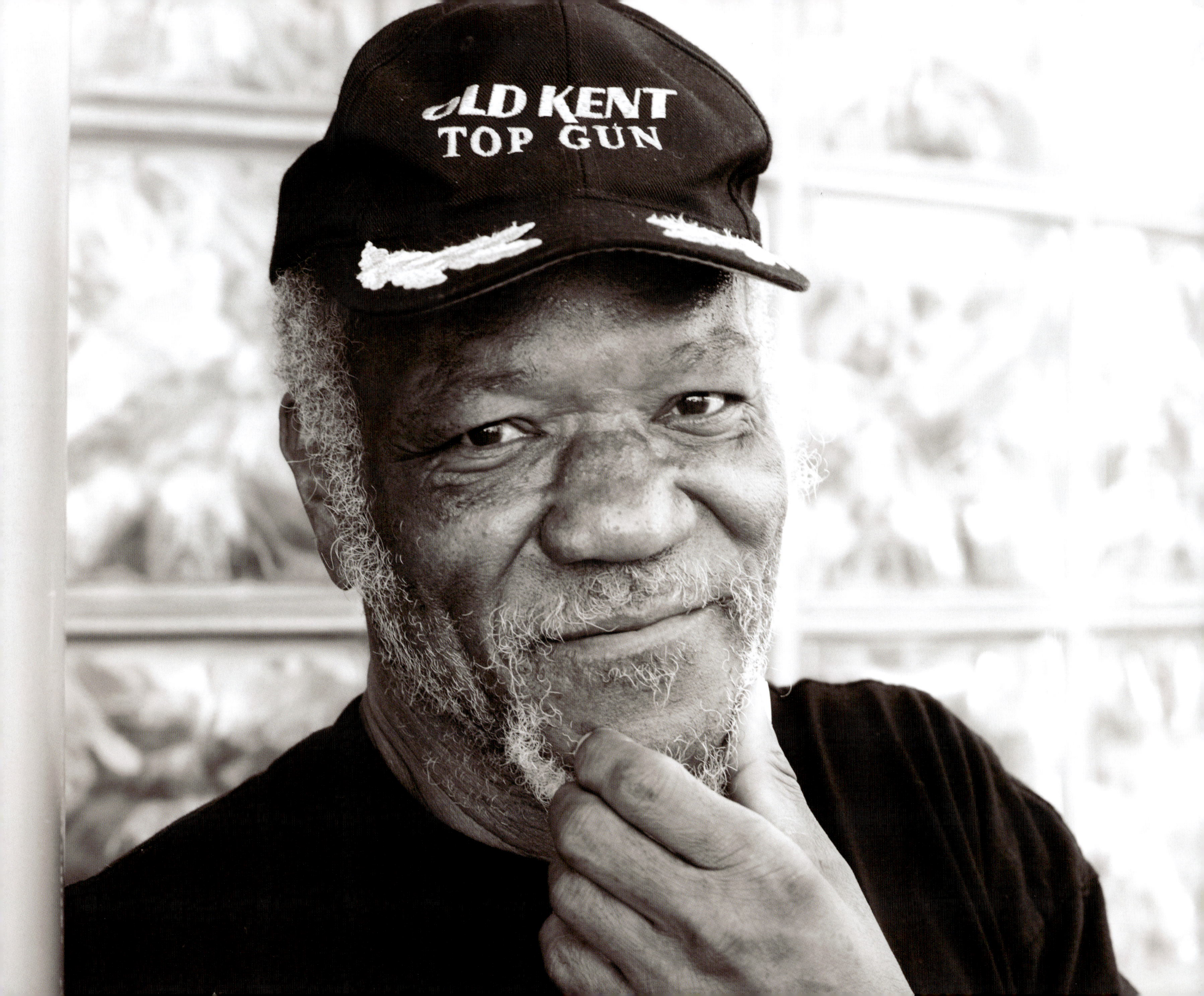
OLD KENT
TOP GUN

EDDIE TAYLOR

Vietnam often made the news, but people were dying in South Korea

Deployment: South Korea
Served: U.S. Army
Nationality: American
Residence: Detroit, Michigan
Occupation: Counselor and supervisor for alcohol and drug abuse

*"My parents were very strict, they didn't let me bring girls back home
and I always had to get home early, so I went to join the army."*

"My parents were very strict—they didn't let me bring girls back home," says Eddie Taylor. "I always had to get home early, so I went to join the army." Taylor, who is now sixty-three, was just short of nineteen when he signed up, and he expected to go to Vietnam. He had been working two jobs, neither of which interested him much, and the military offered a more exciting future, or so it seemed.

At Fort Knox, Kentucky, Taylor became a specialist in communications with Bell Telephone technology. When he finished his training, he prepared himself mentally for a tour in Vietnam. But the day after graduating, Taylor's orders were changed. North Korea had attacked the USS *Pueblo*, a spy ship, and he was soon on his way to Korea instead. Arriving in South Korea, he took an immediate dislike to the place because of the odor from the human manure Koreans used as fertilizer on their fields. But he got used to it after a while and settled in Camp Tiger, the base closest to the border with the north.

"We had what was called explodable barracks," recalls Taylor, "meaning if we had to leave in a hurry, one push of a button would make the whole complex blow up and leave nothing for the North Koreans." Taylor says he hadn't known there was a war going on in Korea when he first arrived there. "Vietnam often made the news, but you never heard anything about the conflict in South Korea," he says. But American soldiers were dying in Korea all the time, according to Taylor, and the papers back home weren't covering the story.

A young guy from a place in the mountains outside of Waxahachie, Texas, kept staring at Taylor and following him around, until Eddie asked what his problem was. "Sir, I don't mean no harm, but you're the first nigger I ever seen," the seventeen-year-old soldier told him. Taylor thought he was spoiling for a fight, until his sergeant said the young man was probably telling the truth. The sergeant urged Taylor not to be too hard on him. The soldier, who was named Joe Lloyd Brooks, became Eddie's best friend.

Eddie and Joe were at the movies together on the day Martin Luther King was assassinated. The two men came out of the movie theater and saw fires burning and black soldiers running across a field. Several of the black guys held primitive weapons and began to threaten Brooks. Taylor ordered them to back off, and the would-be attackers told them that Dr. King had been killed. The black soldiers were angry with any and all white guys.

"We just ran like hell," recalls Taylor.

EDMOND PEPIN

A reluctant member of the Wehrmacht finally switches sides

Deployment: World War II
Served: German Wehrmacht (forced recruit), Luxembourg division of British forces
Nationality: Luxembourger
Residence: Heisdorf, Luxembourg
Occupation: Teacher (retired)

"There are so many things I could tell you—where would you like me to start?
I could tell you about how our way of life changed when the Germans came and occupied us in 1940."

Edmond Pepin lives in a smart care home for senior citizens with his wife, Josette, of more than sixty years. A handsome man of eighty-eight, Pepin has an extraordinary story to tell of changing sides during the war.

Luxembourg was occupied by the Germans in 1940. Although this was not entirely unexpected, the Luxembourgers were fierce defenders of their independent way of life and determined to resist wherever they could. They had little chance of upsetting the might of the German Reich, but when Nazi Gauleiter Gustav Simon, the man in charge of Luxembourg at the time, announced the forced recruitment of men born between 1920 and 1924, a general strike was organized. The Gestapo, surprised by this reaction, decided to make an example of the organizers. After a brief hearing, they shot the twenty-one considered most responsible for this humiliation. Pepin, a member of a large farming family, understood the implications for his young life. Like most Luxembourgers, he considered the enemies of the Germans to be his friends. The news that he would be forced to fight those he considered allies frightened the young Pepin.

His future wife, Josette Hilgert, was among a group of young schoolgirls who protested against the Germans and were sent to Germany for three months of "re-education." Pepin knew his behavior was also being closely monitored. At a soccer match he got into an argument while supporting the local team instead of the German one. Threats were made and he began to fear for his life. In this atmosphere of fear he began his teaching career, which was soon cut short when a red envelope arrived demanding that he report to a labor camp.

It was June 1943, and Pepin made his way to the Luxembourg train station where he and some of his comrades boarded a train to Poland. In late September he briefly returned home but soon learned that the German Luftwaffe (air force) was requesting his presence at a military facility in Czechoslovakia. Pepin, like so many others, considered going underground, but he knew how mercilessly the occupying Germans treated the families of deserters. One of eight children, he was determined to not put his family at risk. Pepin chose to pin his hopes on surviving the war.

Sent to Austria and France over the next several months, Pepin ended up, in May 1944, stationed near Le Havre. It was then, with the help of a French family, he began to makes plans to go underground. But unexpectedly, and unaware that D-Day was imminent, he was sent on to Cherbourg to help man the searchlights that lit up the night skies and detected incoming aircraft. The enormous size of the Allied attack—a total of three million troops—proved too much for the Germans' defense. Many were taken prisoner, including Pepin, who was transported to England in an American truck on June 25.

Finally, as a Luxembourger, Pepin was allowed to change sides and join the troops with whom he felt a natural allegiance. The Luxembourg Battery formed and became integral to the Allied effort in France, Belgium, and Luxembourg. At the end of the war, they stayed on as an occupying force in Germany. Pepin had come full circle during World War II.

Photo Andrew Wakeford

ROBERT F. SHELATO

A memorable encounter with a legend

Deployment: World War II, Europe
Served: U.S. Army
Nationality: American
Residence: Ogdensburg, New York
Occupation: Retired from Ralston Purina and the Shelato mail order business

"A shiver ran down my spine when I realized it was General Patton."

Robert Shelato is eighty-six. On June 23, 1943, he was inducted into the army and sent to boot camp training. Several days later Shelato was called to stand in a single line as his officer walked down it and informed each man what his job would be in the army. "It ranged from being a cook, truck driver, or tool corporal," he says. "When he came to me he appointed me weapons sergeant. It took me a while, but I finally figured out what this meant. I was to provide security for the troops and stand by while bridges or structures necessary for the war were built."

Arriving in England, Shelato began to prepare for battle on the continent. About a month after the D-Day invasion he crossed the English Channel and entered France. It was late summer when he encountered general George S. Patton. "My group was looking for mines along a deserted road in France," says Shelato. "Suddenly I heard a vehicle approaching from behind." Feeling alarmed, Shelato and his fellow soldiers looked down the road and saw four U.S. Army jeeps approaching. One of the jeeps had four stars on it, indicating that a general was likely on board. "A shiver ran down my spine when I realized it was General Patton," recalls Shelato.

As the jeep came closer, Patton gave Shelato the eye, wiggling his gloved hand and motioning for him to approach. Patton asked the weapons sergeant how long they'd been looking for buried mines along the road. "My crew has been looking for about three miles," Shelato replied. "Have you found any?" asked Patton. "No sir we have not," said Shelato. Leaning closer and now speaking in a loud voice, Patton said, "Do you expect to find any up there?" Shelato assured him there wouldn't be any mines up ahead, and with that the fabled general dismissed him. Patton jumped up from his seat, grabbed the Jeep's windshield, and directed the convoy up the unexplored road. "I honestly was a little nervous about telling him that," recalls Shelato.

"Patton made it all the way without incident," says Shelato. "When he arrived at the top of hill, he surveyed the surrounding area, turned around, and swiftly came back down the road without incident." As the convoy drove quickly by them, Shelato and his crew stood in salute until it disappeared from view.

Photo Robert H. Miller

Fr. Patrick Casey

Becoming a mature adult in the Navy

Deployment: Persian Gulf, peacetime activities

Served: U.S. Navy

Nationality: American

Residence: Canton, Michigan

Occupation: Catholic priest and pastor of St. Thomas a` Becket Catholic Church, Canton, Michigan

"Joining the Navy was the smartest thing I ever did. It helped me understand that I wanted to become a priest."

The well-spoken and extremely popular pastor of St. Thomas a` Becket Catholic Church in Canton, Michigan, Fr. Patrick Casey, forty-eight, grew up in an Irish family in a suburb of Detroit. His father was a submariner during World War II, and Casey had thought he would follow in his father's footsteps because it interested him. "I always wanted to be on submarines, but I never quite got there," he says. "I really could not decide what I wanted to do with my life." By the time he graduated from high school, the priesthood was smoldering deep inside him. But Casey decided to join the Navy, believing it would surely allow him to do something positive with his life.

"I really joined to get out of the house and see the world," says Casey, "and back in those days I was a drinking guy and always looking for a good time. The Navy offered me those good times." Casey was almost two years into his service when his newfound party spirit and independence butted up against the discipline requirements and daily regimens of his commanding officer.

I had developed the biggest chip on my shoulder, and my attitude was horrible. I hated the Navy, the discipline, and anyone associated with it. I was mad at the world. Ten minutes before my liberty time, my leading supervisor told me to start a new assignment that would cut into my free time on shore. Being really stupid, I turned to him, looked him in the eye, told him to do something that is biologically impossible to do, and walked away.

Casey was immediately put on report and told to see the executive officer. "I was in really big trouble," he recalls. "The officer ripped me up one side and down the other and called me exactly what I was: a spoiled rotten middle-class white kid from the suburbs who had always had it his own way." The executive officer pushed his face closer to Casey's and ordered him to "grow up now." Casey's penance included lots of extra work. That night, in mental turmoil, Casey experienced a grace-filled moment when he finally realized the truth of what his commander had said to him. He decided right then he was going to change and improve, even if it killed him. This was the beginning of Patrick Casey's path to the priesthood.

Later, in the early 1980s, during Ronald Reagan's presidency, the Cold War was much on the minds of Americans. Casey, with his newly positive attitude, was on the massive aircraft carrier Independence located in the Persian Gulf.

The skipper got on the horn and said there would be two Russian spy planes flying directly overhead in about ten minutes. Everyone was told to grab cameras and report on deck. Eventually about a thousand of us were on the flight deck with our cameras pointed to the sky taking pictures of the Russian planes. Ironically, they were doing the exact same thing—taking pictures of us.

Somewhere in Moscow, deep in the archives, are the photos of one thousand Navy sailors standing on an aircraft carrier aiming their cameras to the sky, says Casey. "To me that's an incredible moment."

Photo Robert H. Miller

JOHN ROBERT SLAUGHTER

As a ranger with the 116th Infantry, he fought his way through France and Holland to Germany

Deployment: World War II, Europe
Served: U.S. Army
Nationality: American
Residence: Roanoke, Virginia
Occupation: Business executive, *Roanoke Times* (retired)

*"You know what a deer feels like on the first day of hunting season—
you just hope it's gonna be a clean wound."*

Bob Slaughter sits in an upholstered chair in his paneled study holding a dark wooden frame in his hands. Turning it this way and that under the reading lamp, Slaughter, now eighty-six, studies for the umpteenth time the typed text and the several dozen signatures that fill every space on its front and back. Looking up, he explains quietly, "they were my buddies," and his voice cracks.

In the frame is a handout of Eisenhower's speech, given to all the men about to hit the beaches on D-Day. For no particular reason that he can recall now, Sergeant Slaughter had asked the men around him on that gray and chilly June morning to sign it for him. Today it is his most treasured possession.

When the men clambered off of the landing craft, the seas were rough all around them. With their heavy gear now soaked with water, most were gulping the salty foam as they struggled to keep their heads above water. But Slaughter, though still a teenager, was six feet five inches tall, and as he trudged toward the beach amid crashing shells and artillery fire he pulled a group of shorter men along with him.

This was only the beginning of what Slaughter calls his "long march." As a ranger with the 116th Infantry, he fought his way through France and Holland, survived the Battle of the Bulge, and pressed onward into Germany. He came home in 1945, grateful to be alive and respectful of those who were not so fortunate.

Fifty years after the D-Day landing, Bob Slaughter, representing the 29th Division, walked Omaha Beach again, this time alongside president Bill Clinton. He later helped memorialize his brothers in battle as a key organizer behind the National D-Day Memorial in Bedford, Virginia, about thirty miles from his home in Roanoke.

Photo Robert Sullivan
Text Joe Fab

AUGUSTUS GRASSO

No longer a homeless veteran

Deployment: Stateside

Served: U.S. Army

Nationality: American

Residence: Detroit, Michigan

Occupation: Truck driver and handyman

"I learned my addiction in the service."

Augustus Grasso does not look like someone who was once homeless. He appears an ordinary fifty-seven-year-old American man. But within minutes of meeting him, it becomes clear that this veteran's pride and pain are tightly intermingled with events from his past. Like peeling an onion, Augustus begins to describe his life one layer at a time. Every new layer he exposes reveals increasing pain.

"It can happen to anyone at any time," he says. "Life's events just start stacking up, and eventually they fall in and around you." Grasso served during the Vietnam War, from 1972 to 1975. He explains that he was one of the fortunate soldiers who never fought in the war. His unit had been prepared to leave on several occasions, but, in every instance, the deployment was called off. "I stayed stateside serving my country from here," he says. "My job was to interact with the returning Vietnam boys. It didn't take me long to discover drugs and alcohol to ease the pain of what I was seeing.

"Pain was everywhere," he says, "because all us troops were treated badly when we returned home or went on leave. It didn't matter if I was there or not—we were all treated just like garbage. America was not interested in this war." Augustus recalls that people accused him directly of killing innocent civilians and babies in Vietnam. He also remembers people spitting on him and other veterans. "The Army uniform was our liability and gave people the opportunity to lash out at us," he says. The lack of support from both the public and the government, which Grasso believes turned a blind eye to the situation, left him angry and depressed.

Humiliation, anger, and resentment fueled his soul, and soon enough Grasso discovered he had Hepatitis C from his years of abusing drugs. Becoming homeless became a slow but steady process for him. "I was married, but I moved from job to job, and drugs and alcohol were controlling my life," he says. "I learned this behavior while I served, and I was constantly high." Because of alcohol and drugs, Grasso could not hold a job, and eventually he was divorced, lost everything, and began to live on the street. Soon he had turned to crime and landed in prison. "After doing some extended time," he says, "I was released from prison and ended up homeless in the heart of the city of Detroit." Grasso became homeless in 1999 and believes that his past as a substance abuser and ex-con, combined with his age, made him an unlikely hire. "It is my opinion that I caused my life to happen this way," he says. "This is what I had coming to me."

As a homeless veteran, Augustus Grasso eventually found a place at the Michigan Veterans Foundation homeless shelter in Detroit. He says that living there and receiving extensive counseling opened up his eyes to an entirely new world that he had "refused to see and acknowledge before. I was too proud and too stubborn, and I blamed everyone else for my problems."

In October 2011 Grasso had been clean for over a year, and he now takes full responsibility for both his past and his future. Today he is living for his family—his ex-wife, daughter, son, and seven grandchildren. "God, I do love life now," says Grasso.

DAKOTA MEYER

The life of a hero carries responsibilities

Deployment: Iraq and Afghanistan

Served: U.S. Marines

Nationality: American

Residence: Columbia, Kentucky

Occupation: Former construction worker

"I didn't want to receive the Medal of Honor and all the responsibility that comes with it.
It didn't take long to decide that I could either embrace or reject it."

Dakota Meyer loves a good challenge. When he was eighteen, in 2006, he had never given a thought to joining the military until he walked up to the marine recruiting table at his high school. His replies to the recruiter's questions were cocky and evasive, and he was convinced he'd had the upper hand in the exchange. The recruiter, however, feeling somewhat annoyed by Meyer's disrespectful comments, asked him what he was planning to do when he finished high school. "I'm going to play football somewhere," Meyer told him. "Yeah, that's exactly what I would do too," said the recruiter, "because you'd never make it as a marine."

According to Meyer, in that instant he knew what he was being called to do. Returning to the recruiter's table, he said, "Let's get on with it." Meyer had been challenged. "That's all that was needed for me to consider doing it," he says. Within months of high school graduation, Meyer became a marine.

In four years of military service, Meyer faced numerous life-altering challenges. But his greatest challenge came during a joint operation in the village of Ganjgal, in Kunar Province, in Afghanistan. Members of the U.S. military, the Afghan National Army, and the Afghan border police came under attack and took cover. Multiple attempts were made to call in artillery and air support, but casualties soon began to rise. Though wounded by shrapnel himself, Meyer left a safe location to enter the kill zone four separate times to rescue trapped soldiers. On his fifth trip, Meyer recovered the bodies of three missing marines and a navy corpsman who had been killed in battle.

Meyer's immediate actions saved lives and changed his forever. Due to the extraordinary courage he demonstrated at Ganjgal, Meyer became, in 2011, the youngest and first living marine since Vietnam to receive the Congressional Medal of Honor for heroism. "I don't like being called a hero," he says. "I did what was needed at the time."

When his tour of duty ended, Meyer returned home to his family's construction business. Pouring concrete one day, he was interrupted by a call from President Obama, informing him that he was to receive the nation's highest military honor. "From that moment on, my life has changed dramatically," says Meyer. His days are now filled with interviews, travel, and countless speeches and presentations. "My life revolves around people that want to see me," he says.

A different kind of challenge faces Meyer as a twenty-first-century Congressional Medal of Honor recipient. "There is no manual instructing me how to act as a war hero," he explains. Meyer, who is now twenty-three, spends a great deal of his time scheduling and planning speaking engagements and answering hundreds of e-mails. A personal assistant manages his life on Twitter, Facebook, and other social media.

Meyer receives a Medal of Honor pension from the government to help offset the expenses of fulfilling his duties to a grateful nation. Random House will soon publish *Into the Fire*, the story of Meyer's heroic achievements, by Bing West. "I didn't want to receive the Medal of Honor and all the responsibilities that come with it," he says. "It didn't take long to decide that I could either embrace or reject it. I decided to embrace it the same way I did when standing in front of the recruiter's table back in 2006."

Photo Robert H. Miller

MARK COPENHAVER

Captured by the Nazis after three days hiding in a hay loft

Deployment: World War II, Europe
Served: U.S. Army
Nationality: American
Residence: Omaha, Nebraska
Occupation: Retired fur cleaner and glazer

"My initial capture and my POW experience were the saddest and most terrible times of my life."

Even though his memory is failing him, Mark Copenhaver, ninety-one, still recalls vividly the horrors of being captured by Nazi Germany in Mortain, France. Copenhaver took part in the fierce fighting at the Battle of Mortain in the early days of August 1944. "There came a time when several of us were cut off and surrounded by Nazis. We knew being shot or captured was inevitable," says Copenhaver. He and two other American soldiers saw the Germans approaching, and in a last-ditch attempt to survive they quickly conceived a plan to disappear.

"Very close to us was a barn with a rickety hay loft," says Copenhaver. "We ran to it and crawled up to the loft. As we nestled ourselves under the stinky, bug-infested hay, the entire loft swayed from side to side. We managed to go unnoticed for three days." Unfortunately, the miserable conditions made their hiding place unbearable. Every day the Germans would come and peek into the barn and then leave. Copenhaver remembers one of them entering every day and repeating the same thing: "wackeliges stück scheisse" (shaky piece of shit).

The three Americans lived off their rations, and every night they would leave the barn to find water. Late in the evening of the third day, the men wearily climbed back into the loft for the night. One of the exhausted soldiers leaned his rifle against the wall, forgetting to bring it up with him to the loft. Soon the men drifted off to sleep. It was early in the morning when the Germans returned again. This time when one of the soldiers peered inside, he noticed the American rifle against the wall.

Before the Nazi could call for help, Copenhaver and the others decided to give themselves up. "We announced in English 'we surrender' and climbed down to the lower floor," he recalls. The soldier must have understood English, because he didn't shoot. "We knew by his eyes he was happy to have us as trophies," Copenhaver says. "This was by far the scariest time of all. From there our lives would deteriorate further."

The men were now POWs of Nazi Germany. The date was August 13, 1944. They were marched from Mortain for four grueling weeks and ended up in the most hideous prison camp in Germany, Stalag VIIA, where Copenhaver spent seven months.

HORST PRZYBILSKI & IKE REFICE

Foes but friends: an extraordinary example of friendship after World War II

Deployment: World War II, Europe	Deployment: World War II, Europe
Served: German Wehrmacht	Served: U.S. Army
Nationality: German	Nationality: American
Residence: Seftenberg, Germany	Residence: Fleetville, Pennsylvania
Occupation: Coal mining engineer	Occupation: Photo-journalist

"I owe my life to you for pulling me out of the fire." —Horst Przybilski

"I owe my life to you for not killing me." —Ike Refice

It was 5 o'clock in the morning, January 8, 1945, a few weeks into the Battle of the Bulge. In Dahl, Luxembourg, a squad of the 319th Infantry was defending Asterhof Farm on a steep bluff overlooking the German border. Ike Refice (now eighty-seven) and his buddies held a critical flank position, and they withdrew to the farmhouse under "overwhelming artillery, mortar, and rocket fire" (as the Medal of Honor citation for the squad leader of the 319th would read later).

On the German side, Horst Przybilski (now eighty-three) and his comrades charged up the bluff in bitter cold, exhausted and weak from exposure and poor rations. First they were in the barn, and then they advanced on the house. The battle raged for four hours. As the casualties mounted on both sides, the GIs resorted to throwing live coals from the stove down the steps on the Germans.

Eventually twenty-five Germans surrendered to the decimated American squad. All but two GIs had been wounded, and one was dead.

Squad leader Day Turner would earn the Medal of Honor for his actions that day. German soldier Horst Przybilski, seventeen years old and severely wounded in his first day of combat, was on the ground and unconscious with a shattered hip. Refice and Turner carried him out and sent him on to the aid station, where Horst woke up and thought he was in Russia. "I didn't save Horst's life," recalls Refice, "I did—or we did—what was the right thing to do. If they were bad, I didn't have to be."

Przybilski healed up in a POW camp in Fort Devens, Massachusetts, learning English and returning to Germany in 1946. Refice, too, survived the war and returned to Pennsylvania. Over sixty years later, the German soldier came to Asterhof looking for the men who dragged him to safety. Through the efforts of the U.S. Veterans Friends Luxembourg group the two finally met in 2005, and now they get together every June at the group's Friendship Week. Enemies, friends—only time separates the two.

Photo Andrew Wakeford

SOMETIMES WORDS CANNOT DESCRIBE
WHAT A SOLDIER VISITING A MILITARY
CEMETERY IS SEEING AND FEELING.

JOHN CIECKO JR.

Force Recon sniper

Deployment: Vietnam
Served: U.S. Marines
Nationality: Polish-American
Residence: Warren, Michigan
Occupation: Retired veteran benefits coordinator, Purple Heart Association

"I was just damn proud to be able to repay the United States for liberating my parents and me."

Born in a concentration camp in Attenkirchen, Germany, in 1943, John Ciecko Jr., sixty-eight, spent the first seven years of his life as a prisoner of war. He and his parents were liberated in 1945, moving to the safety of a transition camp for refugees. The family lived at the camp for four years until they were offered freedom and a new life in America. John and his parents settled in Michigan, learned English, and became citizens of the United States.

John expresses deep appreciation and gratitude to the U.S. armed forces and the special soldiers who did so much for his family during their time as POWs. After graduating from high school, Ciecko was offered a football scholarship at the University of Michigan. Instead he chose to join the U.S. Marines, where he served for ten years. During that time, he spent thirty-eight months in Vietnam as a Force Recon sniper. On his final tour of duty Ciecko was hit by enemy shrapnel and severely wounded, resulting in the loss of both his legs above the knees.

Ciecko came home, where he was hospitalized for two years until he became fully rehabilitated. He has spent all his working life with the Purple Heart Association, located in Ann Arbor, Michigan. Ciecko has successfully helped more than 1,700 veterans secure full post-war benefits.

REBECCA STINSKY

From helicopter mechanic to air crew to social worker

Deployment: Afghanistan
Served: U. S. Marines
Nationality: American
Residence: Lexington, Kentucky
Occupation: Social work student

"I'm very much one of the guys. They say I am a pretty cool dude with long hair."

Rebecca Stinsky loved being a marine. Her father had also served in the marines, and she was always aware of their special status, camaraderie, and proud tradition. The twenty-three-year-old says she enjoyed her deployment as one of four females in a squadron with 180 males. Her "big brothers" accepted her as one of the guys, she says, thinking of her as "a cool dude with long hair." Her official job title was "helicopter mechanic," but she was also part of the air crew, and was on hand to do any repair or readjustment to airframes or hydraulics.

Stinsky's learning process began after boot camp in Parris Island, South Carolina. She spent several weeks in Pensacola, Florida, attending classes to gain intensive training in metal work, schematics, and hydraulics. Previously she'd had no idea what a socket wrench looked like, she says, but she absorbed all of this new information with ease. After two years as a mechanic, she was offered the option of becoming active as air crew, and she became a helicopter gunner. The job is about being the eyes and ears for the pilots because there is so much they can't see; the air crew keeps them informed. At the time, there was one female pilot, but Stinsky was the only female allowed to operate the guns. Before every flight she would check them to make sure they were working correctly, but she never had to use them in a battle situation.

Stinsky's base was Camp Leatherneck in the province of Helmand, in Afghanistan. The enormous carrying capabilities of the heavy-lift helicopter allow it to carry up to 36,000 pounds of cargo that can be quickly transported to other bases. The cargo might be Humvees, howitzers, generators, food, medical supplies, or water. The helicopters can also hold up to twenty-four passengers with fully equipped sea sacks. Stinsky says passengers on the helicopters she served on were sometimes important dignitaries or cheerleaders going to forward operating bases in the long-running tradition of entertaining the troops. She also managed some Angel Flights, the operations that bring dead servicemen back from the battlefields. Most fortunately, her unit suffered no fatalities during the eight months she spent in Afghanistan.

Stinsky left active duty in October 2010. "I miss it, I miss being around my brothers, the people whose company I value so much," she explains. Stinsky has signed up as a reservist and will spend a couple of weeks every summer and a long weekend once a month with the unit she served with during active duty.

Stinsky is studying social work and hopes to become a counselor working with traumatized soldiers; she believes her background as a marine will be a considerable asset, and she looks forward to the opportunity to give something back to her comrades.

Photo Andrew Wakeford

JAMES L. GREEN

POW Japan

Deployment: World War II, Pacific
Served: U.S. Air Force
Nationality: American
Residence: Warren, Michigan
Occupation: High school principal (retired)

"I miraculously healed and survived."

In the words of eighty-five-year-old James Green:

"What I remember most being a prisoner of war in Japan was, when captured, they tied me up to a clothes line with my arms outstretched and then the Japanese proceeded to take bayonet runs at me, threatening to stab me. Unfortunately, one Japanese soldier didn't care and proceeded to plunge the tip of his bayonet in my neck, just missing my carotid artery. I could feel the tip as it passed deep into my neck into my tongue. I bled so badly and the pain was excruciating. It was awful. Surviving this, they placed a rope around my neck and lead me into brutal captivity for four months. Eventually my neck became infected, but after it was drained by a zealous Japanese guard using a kindle stick, I miraculously healed and survived."

ROBERT F. MCDONNELL

A path to leadership begins with ROTC and ends in a governor's office

Deployment: Germany in peacetime
Served: U.S. Army
Nationality: American
Residence: Richmond, Virginia
Occupation: Governor of Virginia

"I owe a lot to the U.S. military for the skill sets I received from them."

Growing up in a military family helped shape Robert McDonnell's interest in serving his country. His father served in World War II and spent the next twenty-three years in the Air Force. "He was a great role model for me," says McDonnell, who is fifty-eight. His father-in-law served in the Marines, seeing combat in the Pacific in Okinawa, Taipei, and Iwo Jima. "I learned a lot from both men," he says. "When I went to college I became involved with ROTC and went through Notre Dame on an Army ROTC scholarship." After college McDonnell spent four and a half years on active duty and then sixteen years in the Reserves, retiring in 1997 as a lieutenant colonel.

McDonnell's oldest child, his daughter Jeanine, answered the same call to military service as her dad and both of her grandfathers. She served in the U.S. Army, including a tour of duty in Iraq from 2005 to 2006. McDonnell is very proud of her. "It's interesting and flattering that she decided to do this," he says. He explains that her time in Iraq differed from his military service during the Cold War because she experienced active battle.

McDonnell's deployment to Germany, in 1977, during the Cold War era, helped to shape his future life, he says. When he arrived in Germany, he became immediately aware of the stark contrast between two nations divided by a massive gray wall. In Germany, McDonnell's commander was major general George Patton, the son and namesake of the iconic World War II general George S. Patton, Jr.

McDonnell recalls meeting Major General Patton several times at an event called "dining-in with the officers." He remembers him as an interesting and driven individual who encouraged his soldiers to visit the border between West and East Germany to experience the iron curtain. "That by far was the defining moment in my life," says McDonnell, "because I instantly understood my mission, and it became clear there were people that really did have a different view of the world and wanted to keep their people in bondage."

McDonnell remembers the guard dogs, minefields, and machine gun nests he observed at the border and the overall impression of oppression he felt with the "iron curtain" in sight. He credits the United States with greatness for choosing to send its soldiers to a foreign land to work and train for three years for a possible war on behalf of people they did not even know. "West Germany was bustling and progressive and actually a fun place to live," he says. "In contrast, Soviet-occupied Germany—well it was dark and oppressive and sucked the life out of you any time you were able to look over the wall."

That McDonnell became the seventy-first governor of the state of Virginia was no accident. Previously he had served in the Virginia House of Delegates and as the state's attorney general. But McDonnell directly credits his military experience and his past commanders like Patton for his success. They allowed him to see, understand, and then act on a situation. "We are all shaped by our experiences," says McDonnell. "I'm just happy I was able to take my experiences and put it all to work for the country I love the most."

PAUL COEN

D-Day medic on Omaha Beach and resident of seven POW camps

Deployment: World War II, Europe
Served: U.S. Army
Nationality: American
Residence: Canton, Michigan
Occupation: Career military (retired); marketing executive (retired)

*"On June 6, 1944, my battalion had fifteen-thousand men. Within six days
of heavy fighting at Omaha, we lost thirty-five percent of our men."*

His eyes flaring almost to tears, Paul Coen, eighty-seven, recalls the horrors of D-Day, reliving his experiences landing on Omaha Beach at 9:30 a.m. on June 6, 1944.

"What I remember most is the confusion during the landing—artillery and mortar fire and bullets as thick as flies," he says. "What everyone quickly realized, as we left the landing craft and headed up onto the beach, was that we had landed in the wrong area and nothing was as we trained for.

"I'm here on the beach, and I am supposed to give first aid and try to save people, and that is what I better be about, and so that is what I did," he recalls. Coen could only hope to not be hit by any of the bullets, shrapnel, or mortar fire exploding around him. He remembers that, after being on the beach for several hours aiding victims, his buddy, also a medic, noticed an American soldier lying several hundred yards up a hill. They both sprinted up to the wounded soldier, dodging enemy fire along the way. Immediately they saw he had lost his leg just below the knee. The soldier had somehow managed to place a tourniquet around his leg to stop the flow of blood and had even given himself a shot of morphine. "As we were placing him on the stretcher," recalls Coen, "he said, 'boy you guys are real gutsy coming up here in the minefield.'"

Coen remembers thinking, "we better figure out how to fly out of here." He and his fellow medic eventually reached safety without incident. "I reacted to everything without thoughts," he says, "in order to survive.

"Most of the time on the beach you were trying to make a decision on those men who you believed had a chance of making it, and those unfortunate men who would not," he says, sighing heavily at the memory. "To pick and choose is a difficult thing to do. I do not think it is possible to adequately describe the carnage of people who are hit with shrapnel or cut to pieces by machine-gun fire. It is just horrible."

Within days of his landing on Omaha Beach, Coen was captured by the Germans. Before his release in April 1945, he spent time in seven German POW camps.

Photo Robert H. Miller

WOUTER VANHOUTTEN

He helped to evacuate 20,000 Europeans living in Kinshasa

Deployment: Zaire
Served: Belgian Army
Nationality: Belgian
Residence: Beverin-Leie, Belgium
Occupation: Independent machinery technician

"They were so desperate that they offered us their daughters as prostitutes for food and money."

In Zaire, dictator Joseph Mobuto agreed in principle in 1990 to a multi-party system. But he delayed putting any reforms into place. He was already in trouble for embezzling funds for his personal use, when soldiers finally protested against their unpaid income in September 1991 and began looting in Kinshasa. Belgian and French troops were flown in to evacuate about 20,000 Europeans living there. Wouter Vanhoutten, forty, recounts his experience:

We gave the people food, money, and supplies, but when no more was forthcoming they pelted us with stones. Some were so desperate that they even offered to prostitute their daughters to us, often girls as young as thirteen or fourteen.

Photo Andrew Wakeford

JOHN DEJONCKHEERE

He joined the U.S. Air Force to learn something new and exciting

Deployment: Vietnam
Served: U.S. Air Force
Nationality: American
Residence: Detroit, Michigan
Occupation: Retired military

DeJonckheere says he looks forward to each new day and enjoys the view of the Detroit skyline from his window.

John DeJonckheere's room at the John D. Dingell VA Medical Center in Detroit, Michigan, looks different from most other rooms in this hospital. DeJonckheere, fifty-six, is a quadriplegic and a permanent resident on a floor that is reserved for veterans who can no longer live independently. He is tucked inside his stark-white bedding, with only his head and one hand visible. On either side of his head are long flexible tubes that enable him to access water and contact the nursing station. Friendly and confident, DeJonckheere exudes an amazingly positive attitude.

"I joined the U.S. Air Force in 1966 to learn something new and exciting. I didn't want to go to Vietnam and I thought I was insulated from ending up there," he says. "Well, as things go in life, I did eventually end up in Vietnam—calling in air strikes with the Fifth Infantry." DeJonckheere says he liked the air force and decided to make a life of it. "I spent most of my career overseas in six different countries," he says, "and this was fantastic for me." DeJonckheere had been a radio operator, and then he moved into many administration assignments, never holding the same job twice. "I was sent to the Philippines, Canada, Iran, Turkey, and everywhere in-between," he recalls. "I eventually ended up in Burma."

In 1982 DeJonckheere's world turned upside down when he was diagnosed with an aggressive form of multiple sclerosis. A spinal tap confirmed the diagnosis, but he was still in the beginning stages of the disease and the air force allowed him to continue to do his job.

DeJonckheere served for a total of twenty years before he was discharged and retired. Still able to live independently and function somewhat normally, Ford Aerospace offered him a job and he ended up back in the South Pacific on assignment. But after two years he could no longer work, and in 2000 he returned to the states. DeJonckheere's symptoms were steadily worsening, but he managed to live on his own until September 2003 when MS gained full control of his life and he became a quadriplegic. For the last eight years he has received constant around-the-clock care.

"You just do not know what life will hand you," says DeJonckheere. "I am very thankful I spent my time with the air force and have seen the world; I am very happy to be a veteran of this great nation."

DeJonckheere says he looks forward to each new day and enjoys the view of the Detroit skyline from his window. "There is always something interesting going on out there."

Several weeks after this interview, John Dejonckheere died, on August 11, 2011.

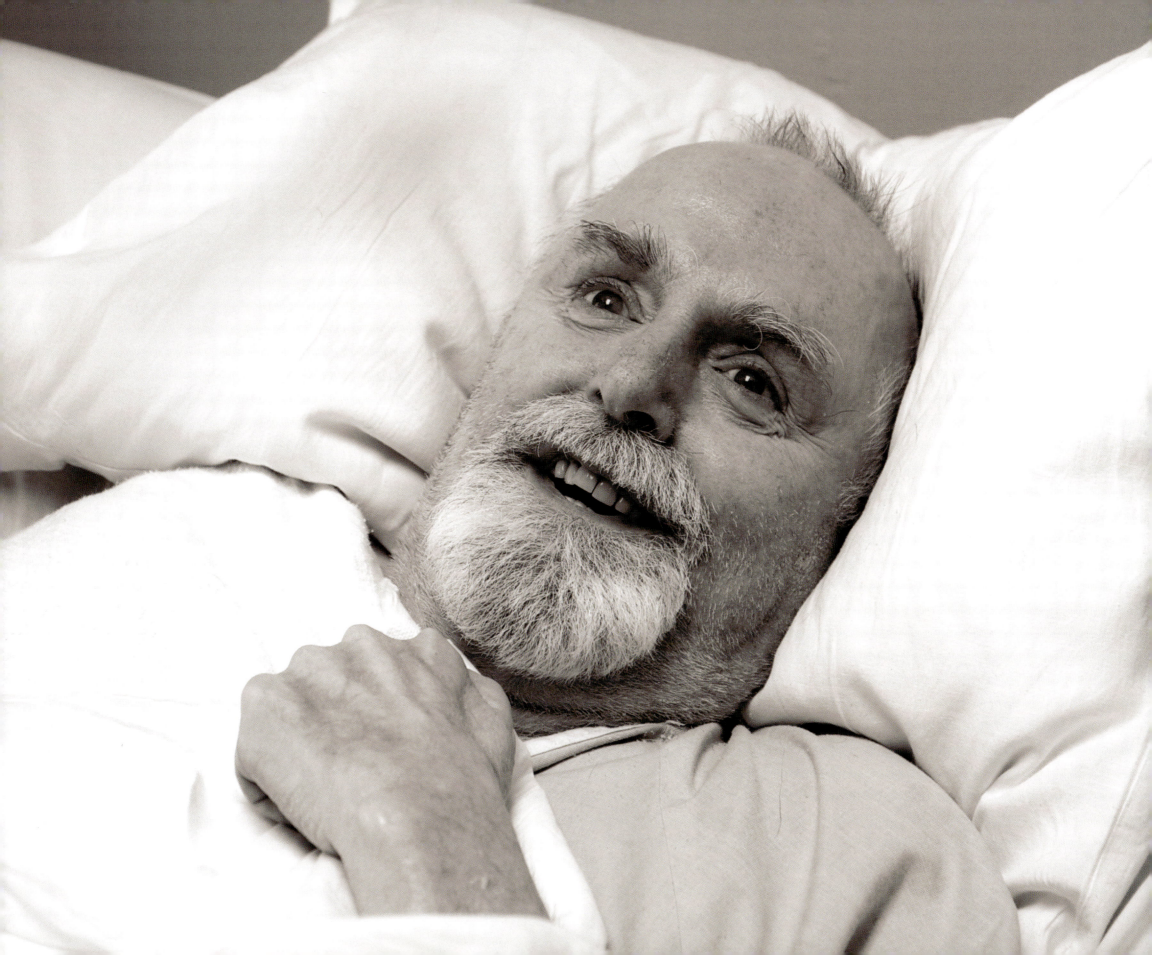

GEORGE "JIMMY" GREEN

His actions helped to shift the advantage in the Atlantic war to Britain

Deployment: World War II, Europe
Served: British Navy
Nationality: British
Residence: Axminster, Devon, England
Occupation: Retired lieutenant colonel, Army Education Corps

"I was twenty-two but responsible for so many lives."

Jimmy Green, ninety, explains in his briskly British accent the confusion about his name: "In my hometown of Bristol I was always George Green. But one of my appointments was as a first lieutenant [he speaks the word as the English do: "lef-tenant"], and first lieutenants in the navy are always known as 'Jimmy the Ones,'" he continues, "so I've been 'Jimmy Green' ever since."

It is a rather undistinguished name for one whose military career was anything but that. In 1941, Jimmy was nineteen years of age and serving aboard the HMS Bulldog. For months the old destroyer had patrolled the dismal seas between Iceland and Greenland keeping watch for Nazi U-boats without sighting a single one. But one day in May her depth charges blew a submarine to the surface. To their credit, the crew emerged and went to their guns to defend themselves, but the Brits were ordered to open fire. At his position, Jimmy turned the three-inch gun on the Germans, who jumped over the side to safety. The Brits picked them out of the sea, then boarded the captured vessel and collected all the equipment they found.

Among the seized material was the Enigma Machine—the machine the Nazis used to encode their top secret communications and

battle plans. Jimmy and his colleagues were told much later that their actions shifted the advantage in the war in the Atlantic to Britain.

Three summers later, First Lieutenant Green's unit was called down to Weymouth, England, where something big was clearly brewing. In early June, he was taken into the resort community's seaside pavilion, which was being used as a command headquarters. There he learned about the imminent launch of Operation Overlord. And in that pavilion, a twenty-two-year-old British seaman was given the complete responsibility for getting six landing craft carrying hundreds of men—the entire first wave—to Omaha Beach, Vierville-sur-Mer, at 6:30 on the morning of June 6, 1944.

It was an extraordinary challenge, but Jimmy Green accomplished his formidable mission. When he tells of that day—on which over one hundred thousand soldiers began their advance into Europe to defeat Hitler—he is passionate about the role he and his countrymen played on June 6, 1944. "Still, today, in Normandy," he says, "people are saying the American navy brought the first wave in. But it was the British Navy and British landing craft that brought those American assault troops onto the beach."

Photo Andrew Wakeford • Text Joe Fab

ROBERT NOBUO IZUMI

A remarkable sixty years in the U.S. Armed Forces

Deployment: World War II, Europe; Korea; Vietnam
Served: U.S. Army, U.S. Air Force, U.S. Marines
Nationality: American
Residence: Barstow, California
Occupation: Retired military

"Some things you never forget. I was shocked to see this little girl in an abandoned house.
She was holding a sheet of stamps with Hitler's head printed on them."

The face of Bob Izumi, eighty-seven, is well known during commemoration events in Belgium for the Battle of the Bulge. Born in California, one of his high school classmates was Norma Jean Baker (a.k.a. Marilyn Monroe). He was among the 120,000 ethnic Japanese and their families placed in internment camps after Pearl Harbor, but he left the camp to complete his education in Iowa. After graduating, he volunteered to join the Army in June 1944, and his extraordinary career began.

Izumi signed on with the 442nd Regimental Combat Team, a Japanese-American unit, and then moved on to the 101st Airborne Division as a paratrooper. The 101st was deeply involved in fighting the Germans in Belgium and Luxembourg during the bitter winter of the Battle of the Bulge. Izumi helped liberate many people from concentration camps and, in May 1945, moved on to Berchtesgaden, Hitler's hideout in the Bavarian Alps. While there, he says, "I was shocked to see this little girl in an abandoned house. She was holding a sheet of stamps with Hitler's head printed on them."

Izumi stayed in Bad Homburg, Germany, after the war, and he served in General Patton's unit at the time of his fatal automobile accident. He also met General Eisenhower, for whom he once stood guard. Izumi describes him and all the other generals he met as "wonderful people."

Izumi returned to the U.S. and joined the Air Force, in 1947, later deploying to Korea to support the war effort. During his time in Korea he helped establish an orphanage for GI babies. The babies were often living in the mountains with their Korean mothers, who were unwilling to look for help; for his rescue enterprise, he received a humanitarian certificate from the president of South Korea.

Izumi also received the Bronze Star for helping to save a downed pilot's life during the war in Vietnam. He had negotiated with village chiefs to cross their land to reach the pilot, but Izumi says he was only doing his duty and seems almost puzzled to have been honored this way.

From 1967 until 1969 he was assigned to the astronaut program at Edwards Air Force Base, in California, and had the pleasure of meeting Neil Armstrong, among others. In 1975 he joined the Marine Corps and worked at their hobby shops for twenty-seven years.

Bob Izumi is one of five brothers who served during World War II. His sixty years in the U.S. Armed Forces includes service during three wars and suggests some kind of record. Appropriately, the Japanese division he served in when he first entered the Army, the 442nd Regimental Combat Team, was honored in November 2010 by the Obama administration with the Congressional Gold Medal for their uncommon bravery and valor.

Photo Andrew Wakeford

MARK A. SPENCER

Ten years at sea on a nuclear submarine

Deployment: Around the world on a nuclear submarine
Served: U.S. Navy
Nationality: American
Residence: Brevort, Michigan
Occupation: Pasty shop owner and fur trader

"It still amazes me that I spent four years underwater serving our country."

In the southern part of Michigan's remote Upper Peninsula, a small but flourishing pasty shop uses colorful flags to beckon travelers along U.S. Highway 2 to come inside. Wildwood Pasties is owned and operated by Mark and Brenda Spencer. Every year from April to November, they and a small staff make by hand thousands of tasty pasties, the famous meat and vegetable pastry sought after by visitors to the U.P. Displayed behind the cash register are a flag and a trophy case filled with medals proudly signifying that Mark is a Navy veteran.

Spencer, fifty-four, served twenty-one years in the Navy and logged ten years at sea working on a nuclear submarine, an experience few others are likely to have had. He estimates he has spent over four years of his life underwater. "My service experience was pretty unique and sometimes scary," recalls Spencer. "My longest underwater deployment without ever reaching the surface was 107 days." He well remembers the following incident:

We were coming out of the shipyard to fire a test missile. Our submarine had a long hollow tube that fit around the missile exit port on top of it. This tube sticks up about seventy feet to make sure the test missile leaves the submarine correctly. We were heading down to our test depth, which would leave the opening of this tube that contained various tracking electronics just above the water. We were about ready to fire the test missile, when all of a sudden the fuses blew on our hovering tanks, causing them to fill with water. Our submarine instantly dropped about fifty feet underwater. While that was a shocker, it was far from over. The top of the missile tube that is normally out of the water was now underwater and rapidly filling with water. This forced the front part of our submarine down even farther. We were almost vertical and continuing to sink into the abyss, when our crew reacted and blew the front ballast tanks open, righting our submarine and causing it to rise back to the surface.

It was the quick reactions of the crew that saved them, according to Spencer. "That's why we constantly trained," he says. "You never knew when something out of the ordinary might happen."

Spencer retired from the Navy in 1996 and returned to live in the U.P., where he was born and raised. Ironically, today he lives right near a large body of water: Lake Michigan. "I love what I do now, especially that I'm doing it on land," he says. "Being underwater for most of my Navy career—well, it was very interesting."

ANGEL GOMEZ

Overcoming a debilitating injury with the help of music

Deployment: Iraq 2004 and 2005
Served: U.S. Marines
Nationality: Mexican and American
Residence: Visalia, California
Occupation: Student in a speech therapy program

"I remember hearing other marines on the radio telling me to get out of the kill zone. But I couldn't do anything. I was stuck."

Angel Gomez, twenty-five, drove a truck during his two deployments with the marines in Iraq. On a late-night mission on his second tour of duty, his truck was part of a seven-vehicle convoy. Shortly after the convoy entered the city of Ramadi, an improvised explosive device went off, and a piece of shrapnel embedded in Gomez's skull. He recalls the experience:

> I don't know how it happened, but I stopped the vehicle. We were still in the kill zone, and there wasn't anything I could do because I was pretty badly hurt. I could only see dust from the IED—the whole cab was full of it—but I remember hearing other marines on the radio telling me to get out of the kill zone. But I couldn't do anything. I was stuck.

Gomez's friend Jessie in the truck behind them pulled up and got out in the middle of the kill zone. Under enemy fire, he brought Gomez into his truck and took him to the base at Ramadi. Gomez passed out on the way there. He underwent emergency surgery to relieve his badly swollen brain. The doctors had to remove part of his skull to reduce dangerous pressure. Today part of his skull is made of very durable plastic. He sometimes feels pain around the scars, and the damage to the left side of his brain has severely affected his ability to use his right arm and leg. Initially, he lost the ability to speak and, like a severe stroke patient, has had to relearn much of what he learned in childhood.

Although Gomez speaks slowly, his speech is concentrated and accurate. Music helped him regain his speech. He was able to remember the ABC song from his childhood and sing along with cassettes of fifties and sixties music his dad brought to the hospital. Six years after his accident in Iraq, Gomez has become an excellent cyclist, and he rides a bike adapted to his left side. Balance was a huge challenge at first, but he has conquered that problem. He thinks about his accident a lot but never dreams about it. He is currently studying to become a speech therapist so that he can help others who have suffered injuries like his.

Angel Gomez was awarded American citizenship for his service to his country, in 2005, three months after the IED exploded near his truck.

Photo Andrew Wakeford

BILL WILLIAMS

Drafted to Korea and proud to have served with many excellent men

Deployment: Korea
Served: U.S. Army
Nationality: American
Residence: Livonia, Michigan
Occupation: Financial adviser

"When I returned home from the war, I was so excited to be back on U.S. soil—the very first thing I did was kiss the ground."

In the words of eighty-four-year-old Bill Williams:

Toward the end of World War II, as many of us were graduating high school, we would try to enlist in one of the branches of service. With the end of the war obviously near, everyone was being more selective. Since I had injured my knees playing football in high school, I was not accepted. That was a very hard thing to deal with, when so many young men I knew were going.

When Korea came around, I was drafted in September of 1950 and sent to Fort Custer. I could go home on leave, since it was only a few hours from Detroit. I was placed in a National Guard Military Police Unit that had originally been part of the Presidential Honor Guard in Washington, DC. Even though it meant additional responsibilities, it was an honor being an MP. When we were sent to Korea, I remember being on a troop ship which was way overloaded—five thousand men on a ship designed for three thousand. It took about twenty days—we went through a typhoon, ran out of water, and had very little food.

The first thing I noticed in Korea was the heat and the smell; they were both awful. I thought it was pretty ironic that the first person I met at the bottom of the gangplank was a guy from my own street in Detroit, Vic Banonis. I played football with Vic, who's brother, Vince, made it to the National Football League Hall of Fame. The next thing I saw was how poor the people were and how dirty everything was. Korea was quite a stressful place, as any war-plagued country would be. For example, my company commander, a captain, had received a 'Dear John' letter from his wife. After spending all day driving around in a jeep with him, I was startled when I heard a gunshot that night. He had committed suicide. I was selected to be one of the men involved in the investigation. So sad, and a painful memory for me.

I am proud of the fact that I served my country when I was called upon and that I was able to serve with many excellent men. When I finally got home, I was so excited to be back on U.S. soil that the very first thing I did was kiss the ground.

Photo Robert H. Miller

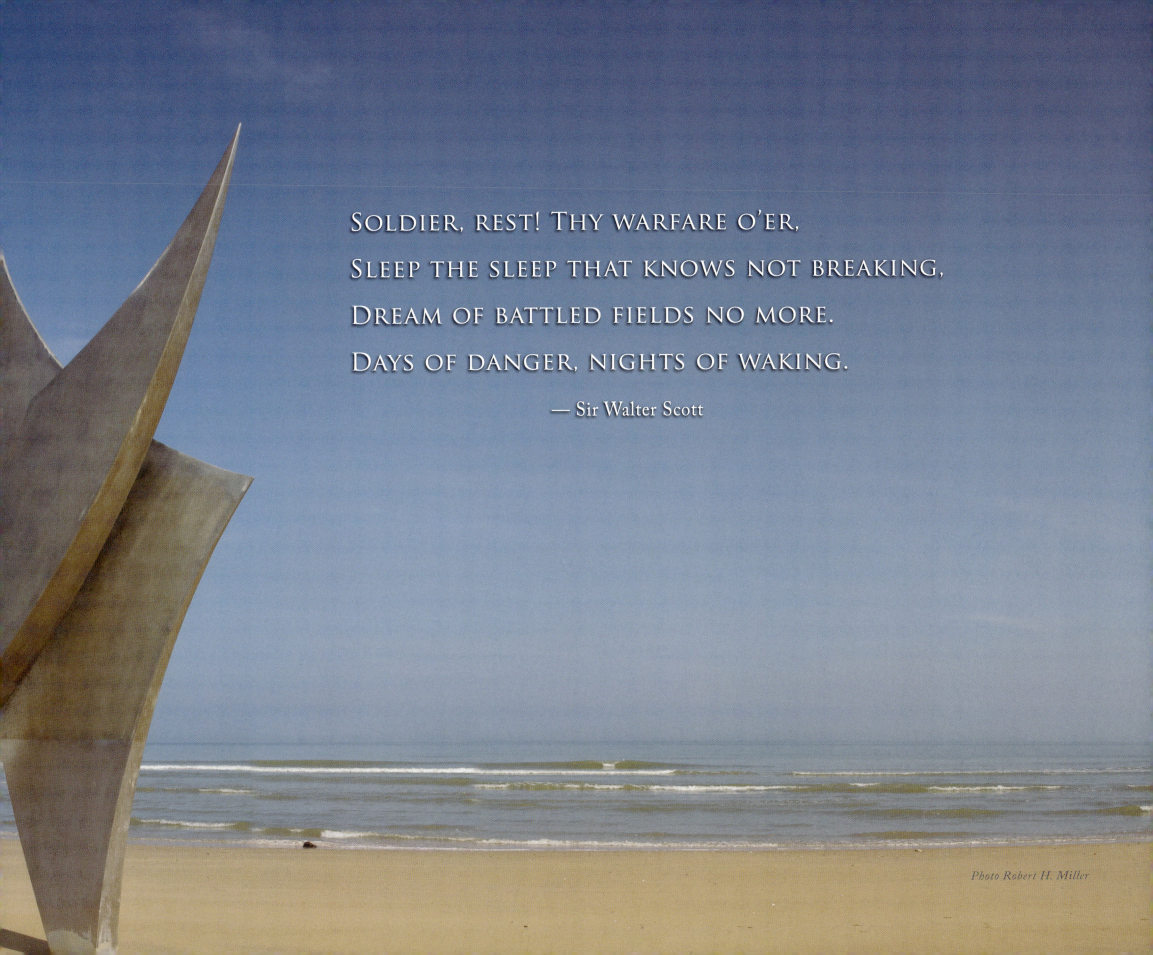

Soldier, rest! Thy warfare o'er,
Sleep the sleep that knows not breaking,
Dream of battled fields no more.
Days of danger, nights of waking.

— Sir Walter Scott

Photo Robert H. Miller

LORD DENIS HEALEY

Lessons learned during wartime

Deployment: World War II, Europe

Service: British Army

Nationality: British

Residence: Alfriston, England

Occupation: Retired Labour politician (Secretary of State for Defence, 1964-1970, and Chancellor of the Exchequer, 1974-1979)

"I was born during the First World War and fought for the duration of the Second World War.
I entered politics to help prevent a Third World War."

Listening to him speak, it is hard to imagine that World War II veteran Lord Denis Healey is ninety-four years old. His keen intellect has remained sharp, and this becomes apparent as Healey recalls his encounters with the extraordinary people whose decisions helped to shape the political destiny of the planet since the end of the war.

In Healey's experience the Cold War was anything but cold. During the years he served as Secretary of Defence, America was fighting in Vietnam and Britain had its own war in Indonesia: the Confrontation War on the island of Borneo, where Britain protected Malaysia's interests. Unlike his good friend and American counterpart Robert McNamara, he refused to resort to bombing tactics. The fighting ceased after four years, in 1966, thanks to considerable help from the fearsome Nepalese fighters the Gurkhas as well as Australian and New Zealand troops.

Healey spent time in North Africa and Italy during World War II, serving as the military landing officer for the British assault brigade at Anzio. He recalls coming upon some surprised German troops still in their pajamas but, on the whole, due to heavy Allied losses, this mission was not considered a success. Too many troops were being deployed in the D-Day landings, he says, suggesting that this was the reason Anzio ended up in the history books as a tactical failure. On the other hand, it is his opinion that the Germans weakened their forces at that time on more important fronts in the hopes of wiping out the beachhead that he had helped to set up.

"Victory in war—as in politics—often goes to the side which makes less serious mistakes, rather than to the side with the greatest positive virtues," says Healey.

By the end of the war, he was moving all over Europe amid the confusion and reorganization that was taking place. He particularly remembers a young Albanian, who had hoped to join the British army to avoid partisan vengeance, bursting into tears when Healey informed him that the war was over. He also recalls viewing ditches full of helmets, webbing, and weapons that had been abandoned by retreating soldiers trying to lighten their loads on the way home to Germany.

The dropping of the atomic bombs over Japan instilled in him a belief in the defensive value and peacekeeping power of nuclear weaponry. On a personal note, he says that this moment also kept him from spending the next few years of his life island hopping in the Pacific.

"No two countries with nuclear capabilities have ever gone to war with each other," says Healey. "Even the unstable relationship between India and Pakistan in Kashmir won't escalate seriously for the same reason."

Healey's six years as Britain's defense minister were the most interesting and rewarding of his political life, according to his 1989 autobiography, *The Time of My Life*. His association with NATO was an opportunity to return to the ideals of his student days and work toward the prevention of world wars.

Photo Andrew Wakeford

STACY PEARSALL

Cameras and comradeship in battle

Deployment: Iraq, Horn of Africa

Served: U.S. Air Force

Nationality: American

Residence: Goose Creek, South Carolina

Occupation: Photographer

"I think friendships that are bound under fire—the ones that I've made in battle, are the kind that are the deepest. You share the highest of highs and lowest of lows, and you can't have that kind of experience on a golfing trip."

Stacy Pearsall, a thirty-one-year-old combat photographer, is one of only two women to win the National Press Photographers Association Military Photographer of the Year competition, and the only woman to have won it twice. She is celebrated for her fearless imagery from the front lines of battle.

Born into a family with a long military tradition, Pearsall joined the air force at seventeen after finishing high school. She's traveled all over the world, and when she encounters a puzzling challenge, she readjusts her life view. Her ability to adapt has influenced her photography. She lives with the painful awareness that her images may be the last photographs taken of those who later die in combat.

"My video partner Katie Robinson is a wonderful woman," says Pearsall. "We had worked together in Africa, and as a reservist she was wondering when she would get to Iraq. She managed to get herself deployed there, and asked if I could come too."

Stacy had more combat experience than Katie and felt responsible for her. "As a combat photographer, you are first an armed soldier and then a photographer," says Pearsall. The two women landed in Iraq and the action began. In a city near Baghdad, where terrorism was rife, their job was to search from house to house and find the makeshift factories that make molten-metal explosive devices. The following day they learned their participation in a particular mission had been canceled. Later the news came in of terrible losses during that mission after a massive explosion in New Baqubah. Armed with

their cameras, the two were allowed through. Many of their friends had been assigned to that mission, and they became sick with worry about the identities of those in the body bags. A phone call came through checking to see if Katie and Stacy had been among the fatalities, because their names had been on the original battle roster. The relief on the other end of the connection was palpable, bringing home how easily they could have ended up in body bags.

Stacy and Katie lost three friends in New Baqubah but had no time for mourning. The next operation was about to begin, and they were assigned to separate units. On the following day a sniper's bullet took out another of Pearsall's dear friends. She set aside her grief and quickly returned to duty. Later in the day, a medic approached to ask for Katie Robinson's battle roster number. Pearsall explained that air force members don't have battle roster numbers, but she immediately understood that her friend had been injured. Robinson's camera battery had been hit, and the explosion had taken most of her thumb with it. After surgery to amputate the thumb, Katie returned to the place she had been shot to rejoin Stacy. "The Iraqis who spoke English," says Pearsall, "said she was 'The Man.'"

Today Pearsall suffers from PTSD and has had to undergo many operations on her back and neck from combat injuries. During her three tours in Iraq, she earned the Bronze Star Medal and Commendation with Valor for heroic actions under fire. She now teaches her skills to others and runs a successful company, the Charleston Center for Photography.

Photo Andrew Wakeford

BOURKE CANTY

A close call that didn't happen on the battlefield

Deployment: Korea
Served: U.S. Army
Nationality: American
Residence: St Helen, Michigan
Occupation: Retired food industry district manager

"My parents would have been devastated if I had died by drinking toxic whiskey."

Bourke Canty, a kind and deeply sincere man, is the survivor of two open-heart surgeries and a stroke. At seventy-nine, his mind remains sharp and clear, but he speaks slowly. Emotion is clearly visible in his eyes when Canty reminisces about his Korean War experiences. He recalls every detail as if it occurred yesterday. Canty begins to tell a story about how he became blind for three days while serving in Korea:

> We were in the bunker, and we were interrupted by a telegram arriving addressed to my friend. His father had died suddenly in America several days back. Everyone felt bad for him. Losing a parent while you were on the other side of the world was incredibly hard. The Army gave him four days of liberty so he could grieve. Adding to the sadness, none of his friends was eligible for liberty, so he had to go it alone. Before he left, he told me that he would bring me back a bottle of whiskey so we could enjoy it together another time.

When his friend returned, he presented Canty with the promised bottle of whiskey. That evening Canty crawled into his bunk, cracked open the bottle, and started sipping it alone. Within minutes he began to feel strange and knew that something was wrong. Reaching for the bottle, he could barely bring his eyes into focus. The writing on the label was in Korean and, with his vision now blurry, Canty held the bottle up to the light and discovered he'd only consumed a few ounces of the spirits.

Canty decided that fresh air was in order. Stumbling into the darkness, he began to slip into unconsciousness. "I really don't remember anything after that," says Canty. "I woke up in the morning with the hot sun beating down on my back." Nauseated and suffering from severe stomach pains, Canty struggled to lift his head. Suddenly it dawned on him that, although he could feel the warm rays of the sun, he couldn't see a thing.

Canty's fellow soldiers soon found him and took him to the camp's infirmary. He learned that the whiskey had been mixed with a toxic poison that could have taken his life. Canty was blind for three days, and it was almost two weeks before he fully recovered. "My parents would have been devastated if I had died by drinking toxic whiskey," says Canty. "Nobody wants to die, but it would have been better to die in battle than the way I almost did."

FRANK DENIUS

Forward observer, 30th Infantry Division

Deployment: World War II, Europe
Served: U.S. Army
Nationality: American
Residence: Austin, Texas
Occupation: Attorney (retired)

"On the night of August 6, the German defenses had 70,000 men and four Panzer divisions ready to assault the 30th Infantry Division in a desperate attempt to seize Mortain."

Frank Denius is eighty-six but appears much younger. He exudes warmth and caring—Denius is a very nice man. But his smile disappears and his eyes fill with tears when he begins to talk about the horrific Battle of Mortain, which began exactly two months after D-Day, on August 6, 1944. Frank was one of seven hundred men of the 30th Infantry Division assigned to hold Hill 314, a mission General Eisenhower had deemed critical.

On the second day of the battle, Denius's commanding officer had become paralyzed with fear and lay curled up in a ball in a foxhole unable to lead or fight. "He was a mess, shivering and nonresponsive," recalls Denius. "Somebody needed to take command or else we would die." Frank immediately began leading the fight against the approaching Germans.

He and his fellow soldiers summoned up reservoirs of determination and courage and were able to prevail in the battle for Hill 314, forever changing history. The direction of the war had now turned in favor of the Americans.

The brutal Battle of Mortain lasted six-and-a-half days, and it nearly wiped out the 30th Infantry, which had held out against all odds. Only three hundred of the seven hundred men who had originally marched up the hill lived to march down off it. Another thirty were captured by the Germans as prisoners of war. The men on Hill 314 became known as the "Lost Battalion." The Battle of Mortain has been compared by war experts and historians to the Battle of the Alamo.

Photo Robert H. Miller

KATIE ROBINSON

The risky and dangerous business of videographing a war

Deployment: Africa and Iraq
Served: U.S. Air Force
Nationality: American
Residence: Detroit, Michigan
Occupation: Combat videographer, Iraq

"A year ago I had no optimism, but now I have some. I want to get better—I want to be happy again."

Katie Robinson, forty-three, has eighteen years of experience as a combat videographer, a job that is nothing if not risky business. It requires spending time in the direct line of heavy fire while trying to document the realities of war. The U.S. military relies on these images for historical, educational, and tactical purposes. In 2007 Robinson was severely injured while working in Iraq.

Robinson has been deployed three times, once to Africa and twice to Iraq. Three weeks into her second Iraq tour, her unit engaged in heavy fighting and the lives of many American soldiers were lost. While videotaping the battle scene, Robinson was hit and wounded. "The bullet tore a path through my arm, destroyed my camera, and took off most of my thumb on my right hand," she recalls.

Robinson was medevaced to Balad, Iraq, where she recovered for several weeks. "I made sure I was not sent home due to my injury," she says. "Being medevaced away from my unit, I felt stripped away and on my own in a very strange land. I was very uncomfortable being removed from everyone I trusted and relied on every day."

From Balad, Robinson was transferred to Bagdad. Once her physical injuries healed, she returned to her unit and finished out her tour by completing six more missions." I had a connection, a reason, and a purpose to stay," she says. "I was good with a camera and loved what I did."

Once back in the United States, Robinson's mental health began to spiral downward. She was placed on medical leave and began to undergo treatment. She is waiting for the military medical board to determine if she can continue to be a combat videographer or if she must be medically separated and retired from service. "It is my wish to stay, but I am unable to do my job right now," she says, "so I'm not sure what is going to happen here. I was the first person to become wounded in my unit and it drew lots of attention. It just hadn't happened before."

Robinson received a Purple Heart, Bronze Star, and an Air Force Combat Action Medal for her efforts. However, she was not comfortable with the recognition. "I haven't processed what has happened. I can tell you that I feel like a failure and that I was not tactical enough," she says. "I should have been more careful—I let my unit down by allowing myself to become wounded. I know this sounds strange, but I cannot get my mind to think otherwise."

Robinson suffers greatly from what she saw and experienced in wartorn Iraq. She still has not come to terms with it and openly admits most of her injuries are psychological. It has been nearly five years since she was shot, and she identifies isolation as the key to her survival. "Isolation allows me to block out all stimuli," she says. "Life is just too overwhelming for me."

Robinson is receiving extensive therapy, and it is slowly chipping away at what is haunting her. She is confident she can have a better life. "A year ago I had no optimism, but now I have some," she says. "I want to get better—I want to be happy again."

Photo Robert H. Miller

GERALD WEST & ROBERT ADDISON

Heavy fighting in the Pacific

Deployment: World War II, the Pacific

Served: U.S. Marines

Nationality: American

Residence: Fort Edward, New York

Occupation: Retired division manager, Sears

Deployment: World War II, the Pacific

Served: U.S. Marines

Nationality: American

Residence: Glen Falls, New York

Occupation: Retired director of athletics, Adirondack Community College

"We went to the same boot camp, landed on the same ship, fought in the same war, survived the same war, and remain lifelong friends." —Gerald West

Robert Addison, eighty-eight, and Gerald West, ninety-one, are inseparable. Their friendship dates back to World War II. "The Japanese bombed Pearl Harbor on the morning of my nineteenth birthday," recalls Addison. "What a happy birthday it wasn't. A month later I found myself in the Marine Corps in a time-compressed boot camp." So many new soldiers were reporting for duty, he says, that their training was shortened so they could quickly be sent on to the Pacific. Addison became a Marine Raider, and at that time, he explains, he and Gerald West "became pals."

"We met in boot camp and nothing has ever been the same for us," says West. "We came from the same town, went to the same boot camp, landed on the same ship, fought in the same war, survived the same war, and remain lifelong friends."

After boot camp Addison and West headed for the Fiji Islands. Neither had the slightest idea what the Pacific theater had in store for them. These two old friends share a significant glance before telling the story that changed their lives and intertwined them forever. They arrived in the islands in the thick of the war. One day their boat incurred heaving fighting as it approached the shore near a small island, and all hell broke loose. Addison and West, along with two hundred other marines, huddled together to avoid the Japanese bombers and Kamikazes taking aim at them and the other American boats in the area.

West tells what happened next:

We saw an American boat that had about 120 men aboard. About seventy of them were severely wounded, and this boat was transporting them to the hospital. Suddenly fifteen Japanese bombers came from nowhere and started pulverizing the boat with everything they had. Addison and I peered out over the railing and saw just the bow of that boat sticking up in the water.

"It was a direct hit and it was just awful," interjects Addison. West continues:

Just as we finished looking we noticed that men were jumping off the boat in order to avoid the fire and residual explosions. In the water in the midst of all the commotion were so many sharks, and many more were heading toward the stricken craft. We could see men everywhere instantly disappearing below the sea. The sharks were having a field day, and anybody in the water would not survive. This was the most horrendous event I personally remember during the entire war. Unbelievable. Who would ever think it would be sharks that killed our men during a full-blown battle.

Addison and West survived to return home, marry, and raise children. And seventy-one years later their friendship endures.

Photo Robert H. Miller

Shawn McKenna

Despair turns to purpose and hope

Deployment: Vietnam
Served: U.S. Army
Nationality: American
Residence: Colorado Springs, Colorado
Occupation: Former police officer and currently manager of Crawford House, a homeless shelter

"No one knows what a veteran goes through except another veteran."

Vietnam was hot and ugly, says Shawn McKenna. Trained in the infantry in 1970, he was sent to Southeast Asia later that year. Enemy soldiers shot at him and he shot back, and then he did his best to forget about it. McKenna does not recall happily this time in his life. He saw a friend cut in half, he saw another one lose his hand, and yet another get blown out of the latrine. Serving his country in Vietnam has continued to affect him adversely.

After leaving the army McKenna became a police officer, but he never again felt part of the general population. He attempts to explain what he means:

> Many veterans, from the Korean War, Vietnam, or World War II, feel very much estranged from our country. When I saw what we were preparing to do in Iraq, I thought, 'Oh no, not another Vietnam.' I support the troops one hundred percent, but what we have done in the name of patriotism is to have guys return broken and, like Humpty Dumpty, you can't put the pieces back together again.

McKenna spent $10,000 of his savings and then in his fifties found it impossible to get a job. This made him suicidal, violent, and angry. Like so many others, he came to believe he'd been cast off. Shawn says that finding Crawford House, a shelter for homeless veterans in Colorado Springs, has saved his life. After his three months there were up, he was offered, to his delight, a job managing the affairs of Crawford House.

"The military want people when they are young," says McKenna, "but when we get older—although I know this isn't true intellectually—we often have the feeling we should get out of their hair and die." In any case, McKenna believes despair can make it seem that way. "In my opinion, when you join up for the military, you sign a blank check for this nation," he says. "Whether you saw combat or not, all of us write that check and take that chance."

Shawn points out a dead stump next to the entrance of Crawford House. For him it symbolizes what the place is all about, because sprouting out of this stump that is supposed to be dead are several branches vibrant with green leaves. McKenna believes it is a metaphor for how this homeless shelter can take hopeless cases and put them back on track.

GARY COOPER

Keeping a promise to a long-dead friend

Deployed: Vietnam
Served: U.S. Marines
Nationality: American
Residence: Detroit, Michigan
Occupation: Minister

"I dreaded to see the sun go down. It was always, 'oh no, here we go again, another night without knowing whether I'll see the sunlight again.'"

Gary Cooper, sixty-four, sees his job as taking his outreach ministry to the streets. "We try to encourage people to do the right thing," he says. "The Lord assigned me mostly to the veterans, and being a combat veteran myself, I know firsthand what they've been through—I have battled with a lot of the same things."

Cooper joined the marines as an infantry man in 1964 and fought in Vietnam in 1965 and 1966. He recalls that the first thing they were encouraged to do was to follow orders without asking questions. He has a memory from when he first arrived in Vietnam of advancing up a hill and then spending the next several nights sleeping on a tombstone. During that first night on the tombstone, Cooper had nightmares about someone telling him to move off and find his own grave. Even today he still doesn't like graveyards, and the sight of white crosses at military sites often brings him to tears.

During his ten months in Vietnam, Cooper, although not yet a man of religion, asked God to help him through a difficult time. On returning home, he felt rejected and not embraced by society as today's veterans have been. Some were spat upon or called baby killers, and most didn't return home as a unit, but as individuals, which made it so much harder to re-integrate. "When I got back I didn't want to be around anything military at all," says Cooper, "for thirty-nine years."

Cooper's marriage quickly broke up, he couldn't go to school, and he couldn't keep a job because he didn't want anyone telling him what to do anymore. Memories of his friends who died after doing what they were told were too fresh in Cooper's mind. He struggled for a time to lead a normal life. Finally, twenty-five years ago, he formed a relationship with God, remarried, held a stable job, and raised a family. It has now been fifteen years since he decided to become a minister.

Cooper explains why it took him so long to get a grip on his life. In 1965 in Vietnam he was manning his anti-tank gun and saw his friend Stanley Kochinsky coming toward him to talk and share a break. Kochinsky was passing under a shady tree when Cooper saw someone else who was walking away from the tree step on a landmine. The subsequent explosion took off the back of Kochinsky's head. The memories of his friend's life draining away in his arms affected Cooper profoundly. He and Kochinsky had promised to visit each other's family if one of them was killed. But Cooper says he could never seem to get up the courage to visit the Kochinsky family.

But Cooper did find the Kochinsky family, and they embraced him like a long-lost son. To his surprise, he learned that they had been trying to contact him for thirty-nine years. On the day Gary Cooper dies, he will know he fulfilled his obligation to his friend and be at peace.

Photo Andrew Wakeford

DANTE J. ORSINI

Franklin Delano Roosevelt's personal guard

Deployment: World War II
Served: U.S. Marines
Nationality: American
Residence: South Glens Falls, New York
Occupation: Retired executive, Scott Paper Company

"I was with President Roosevelt when he dedicated the Jefferson Memorial and when he placed the cornerstone for the Bethesda Naval Hospital. Both were very memorable moments,"

Dressed in a crisp blue suit and brimming with enthusiasm, Dante Orsini appears far younger than his ninety-one years. His voice is compelling, and he speaks of his World War II experiences as if it all happened only yesterday.

Because there were no jobs to be found in 1939, Orsini and a close friend decided to enlist in the marines. But after enduring grueling boot camp training, the officer in charge called Orsini into his office and informed him that his superior typing skills were needed in Washington, DC. Orsini left for the nation's capital, his ego slightly deflated, to assume his new duties. "I just could not believe this," Orsini recalls. "I wanted to go to Europe—not be a typist." It was two years before the bombing of Pearl Harbor and the crisis in Europe was escalating, recalls Orsini. "Soon I received another call to report to my command officer, and that is when he dropped a bombshell. I found myself assigned to the White House guard staff." Only nineteen years old, Orsini had become a member of an elite squad that would be guarding the president.

In fact, Orsini was assigned to become Franklin Delano Roosevelt's personal guard. In 1941 he stood only a few feet away as President Roosevelt was sworn in for his historic third term. Orsini attended numerous high-profile events and formed a real relationship with Roosevelt. "I was with President Roosevelt when he dedicated the Jefferson Memorial and when he placed the cornerstone for the Bethesda Naval Hospital. Both were very memorable moments," says Orsini. "My best experience came when I was on a train guarding the president and we went to Warm Springs, Georgia, for his vacation. He was the most relaxed on that trip—Roosevelt enjoyed life tremendously."

The lives of Roosevelt, Orsini, and everyone in America changed suddenly and forever on the early morning of December 7, 1941, when the Japanese attacked Pearl Harbor. Soon Orsini was standing off to the side of the president as he delivered his "Day of Infamy" speech to the world. "I can tell you this," says Orsini, "I was never so moved with emotion in my entire life. Here was the president telling the world that the United States and its allies were going to take care of those bastards who dragged us into the war.

"The best part of it all was that we did. Roosevelt kept his promise to the world."

FRANCIS CURREY

Recipient of the Congressional Medal of Honor

Deployment: World War II, Europe

Served: U.S. Army

Nationality: American

Residence: Hurleyville, New York

Occupation: Director Veterans Administration Hospital, Albany, New York (retired)

"The smell of cordite in Normandy . . . that is one of the things you remember."

In 1998 Francis Currey, eighty-six, was memorialized as the first Medal of Honor G.I. Joe Action Figure. "My wife says it's a pretty good likeness," he told a reporter at the time. The former Army NCO had never expected to see a twelve-inch version of his younger self, complete with a tiny Medal of Honor, a miniature Bazooka, a Browning automatic rifle, and a doll-sized webbed helmet.

CHERYL KINGHAM

Thirteen years in the military

Deployment: Guantanamo Bay, Cuba
Served: U.S. Army
Nationality: American
Residence: Auburn Hills, Michigan
Occupation: Pre-med student

*"When I was deployed I was sexually assaulted and obviously that was not a good experience.
But in general, I'm glad I served in the military."*

Cheryl Kingham entered military service through the Florida Army National Guard in 1997. She quickly moved up to expanding roles and responsibilities. Eventually, after marrying and having a child, she ended up in the Army Reserves in Michigan and was deployed to Guantanamo Bay, Cuba. Cheryl spent a total of thirteen years in the military, the last three on active duty.

Kingham, thirty-five, is talking about her experiences as a deployed soldier. She breaks eye contact, looks away, and begins to recall the hardest part of that time in her military life. "Unfortunately female veterans go through different experiences than the males do," she says. "When I was deployed I was sexually assaulted, and, obviously, that was not a good experience. But then, at the same time, we get harassed from females as well, and that is what happened to me in my last year in the military." Closing her eyes tightly, and turning her head from side-to-side almost in disbelief, Cheryl continues, "I went through a nasty harassment from a female commander. But overall I'm glad I did the military."

The smile and positive attitude Kingham exhibited at the beginning of the interview has returned. "Right now the veteran benefit is paying for my college, and I am going to school to become a doctor," she says, "and I guess, in a way, it was all worth it."

EARL MORROW

Forced to parachute into eastern Germany

Deployment: World War II, Europe
Served: U.S. Army Air Corps
Nationality: American
Residence: Hartford, New York
Occupation: Retired American Airlines captain

"As Patton passed me, I immediately threw him a salute, and he saluted back. He stopped in a clearing and announced to the gathering POWs, 'OK fellas, I have a war to win—see you later!' And off he went."

Like millions of other Americans, Earl Morrow was starting his day when the news broke on December 7, 1941, that Japan had successfully bombed Pearl Harbor. "For me," recalls Morrow, "it was an instant decision to enlist in the service and fight." On that tragic day Morrow gathered his things and resigned from college. Returning home, he immediately enlisted in the Army Air Corps, the forerunner to the U.S. Air Force. Marrow had always been interested in flying, and he told the recruiter he wanted to become a pilot. "There were no questions—they enlisted me immediately," he says.

Morrow spent a year in flight training school. "It was very intense, and we learned everything we needed to know," recalls the ninety-year-old Morrow. He made the grade as an elite flyer and soon had his wings and his first-lieutenant rating. He began piloting the largest airplane on the planet: the massive Flying Fortress. Morrow and his flight crew were assigned to Europe and flew seventeen successful missions. He remembers that time in his life:

> On several of the missions we landed with only two engines working out of a total of four. On some of the more intense flights, we landed with bullet holes in our fuselage. On our eighteenth mission our good luck ran out. We were flying at high altitude when we took enemy fire from several German aircraft. They sprayed our plane with bullets that hit our engines and caused them to explode and catch the rest of the plane on

fire. Life can deliver some very tough choices—our only choice was to bail out at 28,000 feet. We lost three boys in the back of the plane who were my closest friends, and my co-pilot barely survived.

As Morrow parachuted down he had a front row seat to the fighting going on far below in eastern Germany. "I landed about thirty feet away from three women running at me with large pitchforks," he says, "and that's when the fun started."

Morrow became a POW and then transferred to a Stalag camp near Berlin. But the Russians were coming toward Berlin, and over the next few months he was constantly moved, eventually ending up in Moosburg, Germany, at the notorious Stalag VIIA prison camp. Morrow recalls how the war ended for him:

> We weren't there long—maybe two weeks at the most—and that's when I saw Patton. General Patton's tank and entourage crashed through the gate and liberated our camp. As Patton passed me, I immediately threw him a salute and he acknowledged and saluted back. He stopped in a clearing and announced to the gathering POWs, 'OK fellas, I have a war to win—see you later!' And off he went.

Morrow was now a free man and in less than two months he was back in America.

Photo Robert H. Miller

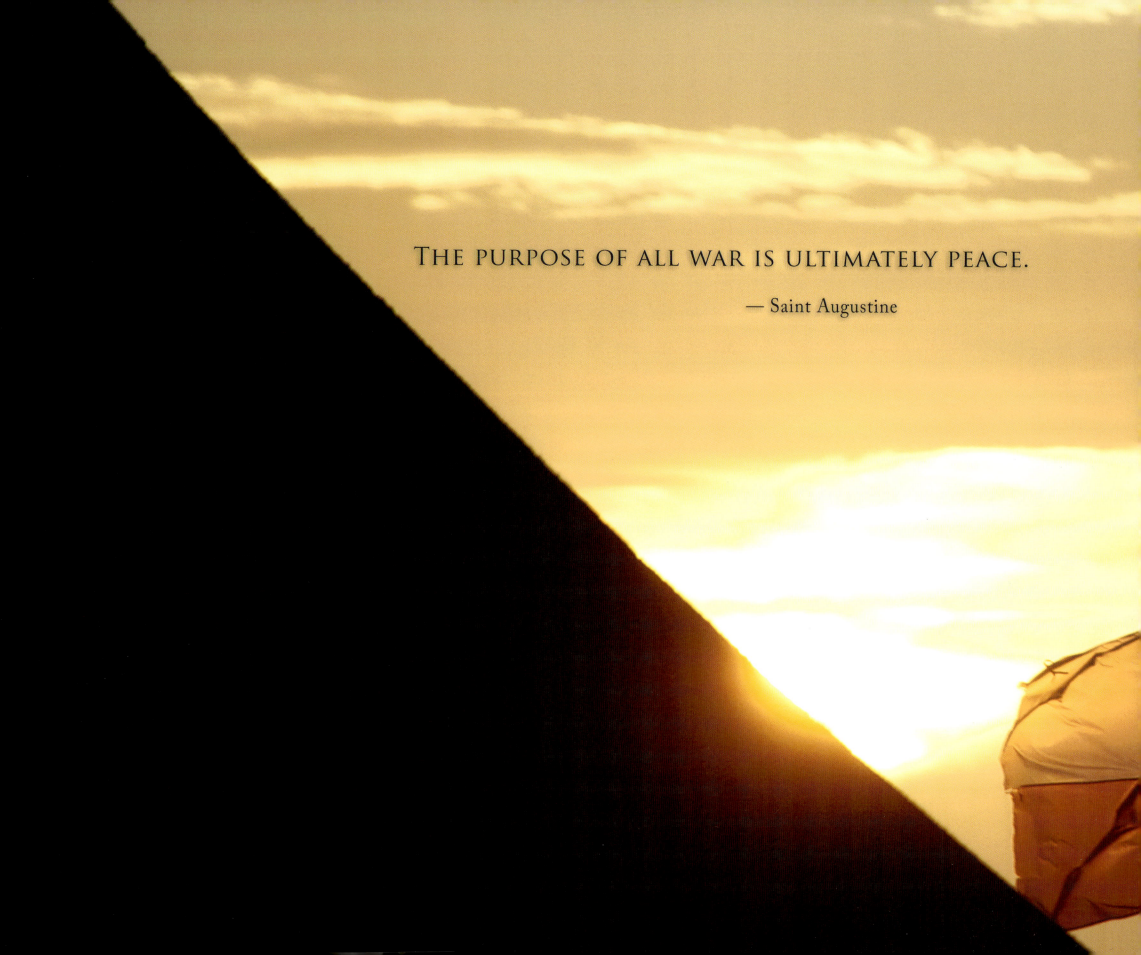

THE PURPOSE OF ALL WAR IS ULTIMATELY PEACE.

— Saint Augustine

Jimmy Lovett

Helping at home

Deployment: South America (2002), Iraq (2004 and 2005), New Orleans (2005)
Served: U.S. Navy
Nationality: American
Residence: Lexington, Kentucky
Occupation: Student studying kinesiology and psychology

Jimmy spent the flight with his arms wrapped around the deaf, mute, confused, and terrified little old lady.

"The relief effort for Hurricane Katrina is not a combat story—I'd already had three deployments—but that's what really changed my life," says thirty-two-year-old Jimmy Lovett.

In 2004 he was on the Monterey, a ship supplying the USS Harry S. Truman in the Persian Gulf. The Monterey took part in surface warfare, specifically identifying suspect ships and small boats. During a six-month period he saw daylight only five times; his job was to fly at night as an air crewman and rescue swimmer. Lovett's deployment ended in June 2005, and he returned to base in Jacksonville, Florida, in August, at about the time Hurricane Katrina struck. When the levee broke in New Orleans, he flew evacuation missions from Pensacola to the city for twenty-one days. This was a new experience for Lovett, who had been trained for over-water (not urban) rescue.

In the early stages of the evacuation, Lovett's group didn't have a plan. But they were experienced and disciplined enough to know how to respond to a situation. He says he will never forget flying in the dark with night-vision goggles and seeing people using flashlights all along the coast, halfway to Pensacola. All unnecessary equipment had been cleared from the helicopter to make as much space as possible for survivors. One night the crew of the copter found themselves hovering above a hospital.

"We were too heavy to land, so we had to hoist ourselves down onto the roof," says Lovett. "I was the one to be hoisted down, and my partner was the one servicing the hoist. These were people who had three stories of water around their hospital and had been stranded for three days." They decided to take the oldest people first. "It was a tough time for me—I weigh a hundred-and-fifty pounds and the first lady weighed probably three hundred." Lovett

got the woman out of her wheelchair and into the hoist and rode up with her until she could be pulled inside. Next he sent up a much smaller lady, who he estimates was about ninety years old. Suddenly the "ship" left without him on an emergency.

The helicopter soon returned to pick up Lovett, but in the confusion the second woman's medical records had been left behind. Jimmy spent the flight with his arms wrapped around the deaf, mute, confused, and terrified little old lady. He was wondering how she was going to survive without her medical records and the ability to tell anyone her name. They finally landed on a crowded freeway and put her on a bus to a hospital in Houston. He's always wondered what happened to her.

On the following day, he worked with a guy he had trained with. This was a good thing, he knew, because they could proceed without needing to talk much. The pilots flew incredibly close to trees and power lines as Lovett lowered his buddy over the water. The level of skill was so high that no one ever really felt in danger that day.

Jimmy's buddy was wading into water about three feet deep when suddenly his white helmet nearly disappeared. Soon he was bringing three people out of a house, hoisting each one up one at a time. He signaled that one person was left but soon came back into the aircraft empty-handed. Soaking wet and dirty, he took off his helmet and sat forlornly with his feet hanging out the door. Eventually he explained that the last person had refused to leave. People can't be forced, he knew, and he guessed that behind the bedroom door was the man's dead or dying wife. Lovett's buddy said he understood that man's decision.

These memories have never left Jimmy Lovett.

Mother Irene Boothroyd, OSB

Helping to patch up 5,000 wounded after D-Day

Deployment: World War II, Europe

Served: U.S. Army

Nationality: American

Residence: Bethlehem, Connecticut

Occupation: Catholic nun, nurse

"When we boarded the Queen Mary bound for Europe, there were twenty-five thousand troops and forty nurses aboard the ship."

In the spring of 1943 twenty-two-year-old Helen Boothroyd had been out of nursing school for nine months and was looking for her first big adventure. Confident and driven, she enjoyed challenges, especially if they involved helping people. At the time, the United States was embroiled in World War II and tensions were high. It occurred to Helen that her newly acquired nursing skills could be put to good use on behalf of her country. She enlisted in the Army to put those skills to the test and was commissioned as a second lieutenant, serving in the Army Nurse Corps. Within six weeks, twenty-five thousand troops and forty nurses were on the Queen Mary heading to an undisclosed destination in Europe.

In early summer 1943, Helen arrived in England and was assigned to various hospitals there. Shortly after the D-Day invasion in June 1944, she was transported with her evacuation hospital, via Utah Beach, to Normandy on the outskirts of the village of Sainte Mère Église. In just twenty-eight days, she and the medical staff treated five thousand people who had been wounded in battle. Mother Irene Boothroyd, as she is now known, recalls the intensity of being a war nurse:

> I can remember being touched by so many men who were suffering greatly from their battle wounds. The scars from war and the wounds received can drastically disrupt and permanently alter lives. I remember this one special fella in England who hobbled out to sit with me while I was on my break. He was so pleasant and nice. Before his time in the

service he had been a lead dancer for the Irving Berlin Show in New York. He lost his leg in battle in northern Africa and was devastated knowing he could never dance like he did before, let alone return to the career he loved so much.

Mother Irene, who is now ninety-two, still thinks about the soldier and wonders whatever happened to him. "I hope he found another passion and was able to live his life to the fullest," she says. Mother Irene doesn't remember by name many of the people she treated. Working so hard to stabilize them and save their lives left her with little time to get to know her patients. "All I could do beyond my medical duties," she recalls, "was to offer them a smile, touch their hand, and give encouragement." During the war, she and her fellow nurses often didn't even know what town their unit was in. "We all were moving so fast to save lives," she says. As a combat nurse, she followed the troops from Normandy all the way to Czechoslovakia.

Captain Helen Boothroyd was awarded five Bronze Stars, one for each of the major battles she was involved in. She went on to serve as a nurse in the Korean War and left the service in 1952. Boothroyd eventually chose to devote her life to God. She became a contemplative nun of the Benedictine Abbey of Regina Laudis, in Bethlehem, Connecticut. In a lifetime of selfless service, Mother Irene Boothroyd, whose name means "peace," has reached out to touch and help so many.

Photo Robert H. Miller

Johny Schmidt

The reconciliation of former enemies is the defining element of his life

Deployment: World War II
Served: Forced recruit and escapee of the German Wehrmacht, member of the *Maquisard* (the French underground)
Nationality: Luxembourger
Residence: Sandweiler, Luxembourg
Occupation: Retired classical trumpeter

"When it comes down to it, and enough time has gone by, reconciliation is inevitable."

Johny Schmidt has a very young look in his eyes for a man of eighty-eight. He tells his story with an expression that combines impish satisfaction and amazement that all this could have happened to him. In February 1943 Schmidt had to interrupt his music studies when, like so many of his compatriots during the occupation, he was forced to join the German Wehrmacht. On leave in October of the same year, his neighbor suggested that he escape to France. He knew desertion was punishable by death, but Schmidt decided it was worth the risk.

To enable his escape, Schmidt had been handed the names of eight people, all unknown to one another. He made his way first to Luxembourg, the capital city, and once there was accompanied to a pharmacy where he was given civilian clothing and his uniform was burned. He crossed into France with forged documents, going through a border post where it was understood that the Gestapo was not particularly up to speed.

Finally arriving safely in France with his false documents, Schmidt was offered the opportunity to either join an allied army or work for the *Maquisard*, the French underground movement; he chose the latter. He came to the small town of Les Ancizes, where he met up with many other Luxembourgers similarly on the run. A group of seven got jobs in a factory, where they were treated well and ate much better food than the Wehrmacht had to offer. Sadly, they were soon betrayed, probably by supporters of the Vichy regime. The Gestapo arrived, expecting to find the seven Luxembourgers at the factory. But two of them were buying provisions in the next village, four were working at a different factory that day, and Schmidt happened to be in bed with a bad

cold. He was warned by another young man in the hostel where he lived and jumped out the window onto a heap of dung. Despite the unpleasant odors he found himself immersed in, he was thrilled to have gotten away.

Schmidt wandered from village to village, until he arrived near Vichy. There a young woman and her two daughters protected him for several days. But Vichy, in Occupied France, was a dangerous place to be during the war, and Schmidt was unwilling to endanger a young family's life. He continued on to Free France, where he was able to reconnect with the underground movement. He later learned that two of his comrades had been found by the Gestapo but escaped execution. The others were found and executed after several terrible weeks in prison. Schmidt well knows it is his great fortune to have escaped the same fate.

Schmidt acted as a saboteur for the Maquisard, helping to prevent supplies from getting through to the Germans. General Eisenhower believed that the work of the Maquisard shortened the war by two months, and Schmidt agrees with that assessment.

Many years later, in the 1980s, Schmidt was asked to play his trumpet at the German cemetery. The occasion was a private visit by the president of Germany, but his immediate reaction was to refuse. He quickly changed his mind, and after this event Schmidt became a speaker for reconciliation among former enemies.

In 1986 Johny Schmidt was awarded Germany's highest honor, the *Bundesverdienstkreuz* (Federal Cross of Merit), and his belief in reconciliation has become the defining element of his life.

Photo Andrew Wakeford

CHRISTIAN BERNHARDT

Equine-assisted psychotherapy takes the panic attacks away

Deployment: Enduring Freedom, Kuwait 2003
Served: German Bundeswehr
Nationality: German
Residence: Recklinghausen, Germany
Occupation: Veteran support group manager

"When I am with the horses, my fear recedes. I believe I am with another
creature that instinctively understands or feels my pain."

In 2003 Christian Bernhardt, a soldier of the German Bundeswehr, was sent to Kuwait to support American troops during the build-up to the invasion. While not officially taking part in the war, Germany was providing equipment, intelligence, and some personnel. Bernhardt's job was to take part in a collaborative effort to protect the local population. Prepared for the worst, his unit was supplied with ABC suits to protect them from weapons of mass destruction, whether atomic, biological, or chemical in nature, and they were told they would have to rush through the chaos of an attack to the protection of a bunker.

Attacks happened frequently, according to Bernhardt, and he says the Germans put their ABC suits on repeatedly, but most of the weapons they were trying to avoid were not all that scary. Bernhardt says he knew how to behave like a soldier and always did what he had been taught, but he couldn't leave behind in the desert of Kuwait the mental trauma of the war. He took it back home. Today he is thirty-four, long out of the army, and he has put Kuwait behind him. But if a helicopter or a low-flying aircraft approaches, he frequently suffers a panic attack. And loud noises are still a provocation for him.

His girlfriend explains how low-flying aircraft at night can still affect Bernhardt adversely. He will get up from his bed, close the blinds, and crawl back into bed without waking up. In the morning he feels drained and wasted, although he has no memory of his middle-of-the-night behavior.

Like so many other veterans, Bernhardt suffers from depression. The worldwide focus on terrorism has left him with an empty feeling. In retrospect, he can't justify his time in the army. With the death of Osama Bin Laden, he believes the war on terrorism is over.

Bernhardt often has panic attacks, and conventional therapy has not helped to relieve them. But he has discovered Equine-assisted psychotherapy, which is trauma relief through working with horses. It has improved his quality of life, and he explains:

When I am with the horses, my fear recedes. I believe I am with another creature that instinctively understands or feels my pain. My responsibility as a cog in the machinery of war has caused me great anxiety and heart-searching, going against many of my principles and having in my view solved nothing. I feel the non-judgmental acceptance of the horses and it helps to rekindle my spirit.

Germain Lorier

A career soldier remembers

Deployment: Indochina
Served: French Air Force
Nationality: French
Residence: Mortain, Normandy, France
Occupation: French Air Force (retired)

"I will never forget the face of the little boy who then lost his only protector, his grandfather."

A flight mechanic and career soldier, Germain Lorier, now eighty, fought in Indochina in 1952. At the time Indochina was an area that had been colonized by the French in the nineteenth century, and it included the modern-day countries of Cambodia, Laos, and Vietnam. The conflict in this region was later taken over by the Americans.

While evacuating the Vietnamese people from the north, where the Vietminh (Vietcong) were gaining ever more influence, Lorier recalled one scene in particular:

I saw an old man with a cane—he was holding his grandson's hand and pulling him along. The little boy didn't understand what was going on or realize the urgency of their mission. Later on, I asked what had happened to them, and a comrade told me that the grandfather didn't survive evacuation. I will never forget the face of that little boy who lost his only protector, and I often wondered what happened to him.

Photo Andrew Wakeford and Robert H. Miller

BUSTER SIMMONS

The youngest first sergeant in the entire Army in 1944

Deployment: World War II, Europe
Served: U.S. Army
Nationality: American
Residence: Farmington, Arkansas
Occupation: Retired sales executive for a trucking firm

"There is no actor who can capture the distress of a dying young man repeatedly calling for his mother, knowing he will never return home to see her again."

At eighty-nine Buster Simmons is quick and witty. But Simmons is hiding many dark memories inside that he would prefer to forget. Confined to a wheel chair after recent hip surgery, Simmons has recovered enough to share a story about his war.

"I was in the Thirtieth Infantry Division and at nineteen was promoted to first sergeant in the medical attachment," says Simmons. "I was the youngest first sergeant in the entire United States Army in 1942." Simmons continues:

At the Battle of Mortain I had my first real emotional test as a medic. I remember him so clearly. His name was Pettigrew—Billy Pettigrew. During this intense battle in August 1944, Pettigrew was wounded in the neck and upper chest, right near the collarbone, by flying shrapnel. As the

shrapnel entered his body it bounced around inside of him causing massive internal damage. When we were finally able to reach him, Pettigrew knew he was dying. We knew, too—it was a gut-wrenching moment.

Simmons pauses, fights back tears, and carefully picks his words. "There is no actor who can capture the horrible distress of a dying young man repeatedly calling for his mother, knowing he will never return home to see her again."

Pettigrew eventually slipped away on Hill 314, despite the care and compassion he had received from Simmons. "Ironically, Pettigrew was a big, solidly-built man," recalls Simmons. "This made his crying pleas for his mother even harder to hear. I was never in my life so moved with pity—it still wrenches my heart with sorrow even after sixty-seven years."

Photo Robert H. Miller

Kathy Jo Benabides

Service in Iraq

Deployment: Iraq
Served: U.S. Army
Nationality: American
Residence: Currently stationed in Ramstein, Germany
Occupation: Military policewoman

"Although I was touched by their prayers for the injured man . . . I was shocked that it stopped them from calling for help."

"To me, Kuwait—that was a real culture shock," says Kathy Jo Benabides, twenty-nine, who was deployed there as a member of the Military Police. Driving in a convoy, she saw that an accident had happened. In front of her was an overturned truck, and the injured driver was lying by the side of the road. Rushing to help, she was stopped by local people, who surrounded the man for half an hour. During that time, they were praying for him, but they didn't call for help until the thirty minutes were up. According to belief, it is Allah's will whether someone dies or survives after an accident, says Benabides. If Allah lets someone live for a half hour, he will let him continue to live on afterward.

"Although I was touched by their prayers and piety for the injured man," recalls Benabides, "I was shocked that it stopped them from calling for help. After an accident, it is vital that help comes as quickly as possible, and I was unable to do anything but wait. I don't know if the poor man survived, but I have my doubts."

Photo Andrew Wakeford

Stephen Hambrook

Traveling the world defusing bombs and mines

Deployment: Northern Ireland, Malta, North Africa, the Falkland Islands
Served: British Royal Engineers
Nationality: British
Residence: Canterbury, England
Occupation: Retired military

"My two daughters told a journalist I was getting an award for putting up with them growing up!"

Stephen Hambrook, seventy-eight, is a former British army major and veteran of many conflicts. It was inevitably his job to clean up after the wars were over, or nearly over. Many of his assignments were extremely dangerous: for example, in 1969, he helped defuse a 250-kilogram bomb, which had been buried since 1941 in Petworth, in the County of Sussex, in southeastern England.

For that delicate task, the surrounding area first had to be evacuated. Next a twenty-foot shaft had to be dug, and after five days' effort Hambrook and his commanding officer located the bomb. With the help of an electric stethoscope, they determined that it was no longer ticking and immunized the fuse, carefully removing it before the bomb could explode. The most dangerous part of the operation was taking out nine liters of nitroglycerine by hand, a twenty-nine-hour undertaking.

Hambrook and a colleague also defused another large World War II bomb in a North London housing complex in 1969. The complex honored the men by naming two housing blocks after them. Their daring efforts in that year were so significant that both were presented, in 1970, with the George Medal, a prestigious civilian award created by King George VI in 1941 and granted in recognition of acts of great bravery.

Years later, after working in military diving schools all over the world, including heading a diving school in Kiel, Germany, Hambrook was sent to the Falkland Islands. It was October 1982, and after the brief war there many dangerous bombs and mines needed to be removed. In January 1983 he stepped on a mine in an area that had been previously declared safe and lost part of his left leg. One moment he was a veteran cross-country runner, the next an invalid. He pulled himself together, as he modestly put it, and served for another ten years in bomb disposal for the Royal Engineers.

Hambrook remembers butterfly bombs in Malta, colorful little toy-like objects that easily exploded if tampered with. He recalls, while on duty one day, discovering a child's bomb-mutilated body, its severed foot in a sandal. It is an image that continues to haunt him.

For his expertise and willingness to travel the world defusing bombs and mines, Hambrook was awarded an MBE (Member of the British Empire), one of the highest awards given in the United Kingdom. "While accepting my award from the Queen in Buckingham Palace," he recalls, "my two daughters waiting outside were asked by a journalist what I was getting it for. They told him that I'd said it was for putting up with the two of them growing up!"

Photo Andrew Wakeford

ANDY DUNAWAY

Living life to the fullest as a combat photographer

Deployment: All over the world

Served: U.S. Air Force

Nationality: American

Residence: Charleston, South Carolina

Occupation: Photographer and partner in a photography studio

"To me if death happens—it happens. If it's your day then it's your day, and there is nothing you can do about it."

The detonation of an improvised explosive device greeted combat photographer Andy Dunaway two weeks into his first deployment to Iraq, in 2005. It was an unexpected and violent welcome. Dunaway had been traveling back from a scouting patrol near the Syrian border when his Stryker military vehicle exploded, instantly turning into a twisted pile of metal. Luckily, all the men inside were able to walk away with minor scratches and injuries. "The two-million-dollar vehicle saved our life, and it was worth every penny that the military spent on it," says Dunaway.

Dunaway, forty-three, is a seasoned veteran, and he is very specific about his career in the military. "I spent twenty-three years and thirteen days as a combat photographer," he says. During that time Dunaway traveled the world with his camera. He shot photos on the battlefield, created formal portraits of officers, and provided the Air Force with strategic photos to be used for presidential briefings.

"Every day was a different and interesting assignment," he recalls. "My job was to document everything possible. My normal day was taking hundreds of pictures and returning to our camp to process film—back in the old days—or download digital images." Dunaway was required to get signed releases, and then the photos he had taken would go to the appropriate military personnel for review. His most enjoyable task, he says, was taking photos of the many diverse things that soldiers do and

then giving them to the soldiers. "These images help build morale and conversations," he says, "and the approved pictures were often shared with families back home."

Dunaway especially remembers the Wall of Heroes he encountered while deployed in Kirkuk, Iraq, in 2005, 2007, and 2009. It represented all of the soldiers killed in the line of duty. It would be updated within one hour or so of any tragedy. The wall was graphic, with detailed descriptions on how each soldier died, the location of their death, and the conditions leading up to it. It was a sad place to visit, and Dunaway remembers this story:

My partner, who we nicknamed Fish, was so overly concerned about the safety of missions that he would read everything on the Wall of Heroes. He actually thought this would help prepare him and prevent a tragedy. Fish became so paranoid that he would walk up and down the vehicle line-up before going on a patrol to make sure he was not sitting on the side of the vehicle where the gas tank was located. His reasoning was that he did not want to catch on fire if struck by an IED. This paranoia really took over a commanding place in his head and became a big problem for him. To me, if death happens—it happens. If it's your day, then it's your day, and there is nothing you can do about it. I never ever thought about death like Fish did. I'm focused on life and living it to the very fullest.

WILLIAM BUREAU

He helped evacuate more than 2,000 people without casualties

Deployment: Zaire
Served: Belgian Army
Nationality: Belgian
Residence: Wepion, Belgium
Occupation: Retired military

"If you have been to war, it is something you would rather not think about."

Asked to recall something still fresh in his memory that had happened during the 1978 war in Zaire, William Bureau, a tough man, immediately has tears in his eyes and says he has nothing he wants to say. "If you have been to war, it is something you would rather not think about," Bureau explains. On a lighter note, he mentions that dictator Joseph Mobuto was so hated in Zaire that people would use an image of his face as a target in weapon practice. He recalls the sounds of different weapons, reproducing them for us at the table with reasonable accuracy, as far as anyone can tell.

Bureau, now fifty-two, changes his mind and begins to reminisce. On the night of May 11, 1978, former policemen from Katanga, commanded by General Nathaniel Mbumba, head of the National Front for the liberation of Congo (FNLC), tried for the second time to destabilize the regime of General Mobuto. They invaded the town of Kolwezi, in the Shaba region, with the support of much of its people. Despite the wealth of this area, most of its population lived in abject poverty. The FNLC rebels attacked Zaire officials and the Europeans who lived there. A lack of discipline among Mbumba's troops and abuse of alcohol led to massacres, summary executions, and rape.

This was the political climate when Belgian paratroopers were called in to help hold onto the airport in Kolwezi for seventy-two hours. The objective was to protect the people threatened and bring them to the safety of the airport. All serious calls for help were to be acted on. If hostages were taken, the Belgians had the authority to take any actions necessary to free them, including evacuating them to Lusaka or Ndolo.

Arriving in the early evening of May 19, the paratroopers had been under way from Belgium for twenty-five hours and were due to leave the next morning, May 20, at 5:30, to jump from the Hercules C130 an hour later near Kolwezi.

"My group was making for the Kolwezi train station by the shortest route, using the rails as guidance," recalls Bureau. "We saw a number of open goods wagons, everything was calm, or seemed to be, as we continued to advance." In the shelter of the wagons, they found their way to the station building. "Pak, pak, pak, bong, bong, bong was all around us," says Bureau. They heard the wagons crashing into each other, and bullets ricocheted around them and pierced the metal of the goods trucks.

During this operation, the Belgian paratroopers evacuated some 2,300 people without any casualties from foreign nationals or the local population. Only one paratrooper died.

"War, no matter whether long or short, lost or won, is a horror, whenever it takes place," says Bureau. "To see it on the screen with special effects is one thing," he says, "but for those who have experienced war, the smell is always with you and the memories of the blood and body parts stay with you for life." Bureau believes that wars are mostly fought by people who don't know each other, and he is certain that those who know one another well will not fight.

"In action, there is no room for emotions or feelings," says Bureau, "your age, gender, or ethnic group makes no difference."

DANIEL LAWLER

The force of the Hiroshima blast shook the island of Okinawa

Deployment: World War II, Pacific

Served: U.S. Marines

Nationality: American

Residence: Hudson Falls, New York

Occupation: Retired baker

"Suddenly I felt the entire island move and sway beneath me, causing my pen to skip across the page. Everything that was hanging was now swinging back and forth."

At eighty-five Daniel Lawler is soft-spoken and eager to share his many stories of the time he spent in the Pacific during World War II. "I joined the Marines on November 8, 1943, and had all the usual intensive training to prepare me for the perils of war," he says. "Basically they took me from a boy to a man."

Soon after finishing up his training, Lawler arrived in Peleliu, an island in the Pacific then heavily occupied by the Japanese. He went in on the first assault wave. "The United States was just not ready for any type of war. We were using machine guns from World War I that were made in 1919," he recalls. They used these same guns all the way through the war, he says, and amazingly they continued to work. On the second day of the invasion Lawler was near an exploding shell that nearly took his life. It landed behind him, and the force of the blast broke one of his arms and the fingers and thumb on one of his hands. He also sustained shrapnel injuries to his back.

Lawler spent six weeks on a Red Cross hospital ship recovering from his injuries. The ship was so cramped, he says, that the many marines who died in battle had to be buried off the back of the ship to make room for the living.

Lawler was sent next to Okinawa, Japan. "There was a cave and there were civilians hiding deep inside it," he recalls. "Holding our guns on target, we forced them to come out and surrender. Suddenly there appeared a little girl and boy tightly holding hands. They were about seven years old. Her dress was bloody, their hair was matted, and they were covered with thick black dirt. These children we terrified." Lawler and the others quickly lowered there guns and noticed that the children were starving to death. He immediately picked up the little girl and another solider picked up the boy, and they moved them to safety. "We all started to cry when we noticed what bad shape they were in," says Lawler. "To this day I have no idea what happened to those beautiful children. Obviously they must have been orphans."

A while later near the end of the war, Lawler was busy writing a letter home. "Suddenly I felt the entire island move and sway beneath me, causing my pen to skip across the page," he recalls. "Everything that was hanging was now swinging back and forth." Totally shocked and almost in a panic, Lawler and his fellow soldiers began looking for safe cover. It was August 6, 1945.

They soon found out that America had dropped the first atomic bomb on Hiroshima. The force of the blast had clearly been felt on Okinawa. Three days later, it was déjà vu all over again when the second bomb was dropped on Nagasaki. "This time we knew what is was," says Lawler. "The war was over."

All wars are civil wars,
because all men are brothers.

— Francois Fenelon